ESSENTIALS
of Business Process
Outsourcing

Essentials Series

The Essentials Series was created for busy business advisory and corporate professionals. The books in this series were designed so that these busy professionals
can quickly acquire knowledge and skills in core business areas.

Each book provides need-to-have fundamentals for those professionals
who must:

- Get up to speed quickly, because they have been promoted to a new
  position or have broadened their responsibility scope
- Manage a new functional area
- Brush up on new developments in their area of responsibility
- Add more value to their company or clients

Other books in this series include:

For more information on any of the above titles, please visit *www.wiley.com*.

ESSENTIALS
of Business Process
Outsourcing

Thomas N. Duening
Rick L. Click

John Wiley & Sons, Inc.

Copyright © 2005 by John Wiley & Sons, Inc., Hoboken, New Jersey. All rights reserved.

Published simultaneously in Canada.

For general information on our other products and services, or technical support, please contact our Customer Care Department within the United States at 800-762-2974, outside the United States at 317-572-3993 or fax 317-572-4002.

Wiley also publishes its books in a variety of electronic formats. Some content that appears in print may not be available in electronic books.

For more information about Wiley products, visit our Web site at *www.wiley.com*.

Library of Congress Cataloging-in-Publication Data:
Duening, Thomas N.
   Essentials of business process outsourcing / Thomas N. Duening, Rick L. Click.
      p.   cm.   —(Essentials series)
   Includes index.
   ISBN 0-471-70987-5 (pbk.)
      1. Contracting out.   I. Click, Rick L.   II. Title.   III. Series.
   HD2365.D84 2005
   658.4′058—dc22

                                                                    2004025808

Printed in the United States of America

10 9 8 7 6 5 4 3 2 1

Contents

Preface

Business process outsourcing (BPO) has emerged as one of the leading business and economic issues of our time. A natural extension of the free-trade movement that has been a dominant force in global economics over the past two decades, BPO has been met with mixed reactions. Workers whose lives have been disrupted because their jobs have been outsourced to lower-wage workers overseas have understandably decried "offshoring" as a threat to their way of life. Others, especially those in the foreign locations where new jobs are rapidly being created, are elated finally to have an opportunity to gainfully deploy their hard-earned skill sets.

In this book, we attempt to examine BPO from the perspective of its application and implementation in businesses of all sizes. We do not address the political or economic controversies swirling around outsourcing. Instead, we assume that the movement of service work to lowest-cost providers, no matter where they may reside, will continue in some form in the coming years. It seems unlikely that new barriers will be erected that will seriously limit global free trade. With that in mind, we have developed a rigorous methodology that businesses can use to analyze the outsourcing opportunity, to make informed decisions about choosing a vendor, and to manage change and execute an outsourcing project.

The team-based approach to BPO project analysis and management that we recommend is based on the fact that BPO is a sociotechnical phenomenon. That is, a well-executed outsourcing project must involve both social and technical resources of the organization. BPO is transformational to the organization and requires attention to the social and human impacts that accompany business transformation. At the same time, one of the primary enablers of BPO is the set of technologies that has emerged to connect the world in a global communications network. As a sociotechnical phenomenon, effective BPO management requires a diverse skill set that is not likely to be present in a single individual. Thus, we recommend a team-based approach since the necessary skills are more likely to be available in a group of people united to achieve common objectives.

We also develop the concept of the BPO Life Cycle to denote clear milestones in development of the BPO project, and to provide more specific management and leadership guidelines to be applied at different stages of the Life Cycle. The BPO Life Cycle applies to any type of outsourcing project, and to any size company.

It has become clear that BPO provides far more than mere cost savings to firms that use it. BPO has become a strategic business choice that can be leveraged for competitive advantage as well. When a business outsources a process to a vendor whose core competence is centered on that process, the buyer is likely to experience service enhancements that can be turned into competitive advantages over rivals. Furthermore, when the buyer–vendor relationship evolves into a business partnership, both sides will be motivated to look for mutually beneficial ways to leverage the combined asset pool.

As this book is going to press, outsourcing has become an important new force in the global economy. It is our hope that the prescriptions, guidelines, concepts, and tools provided in this book will be useful to executives in organizations of all sizes as they struggle to determine their best opportunities for outsourcing. With the rapid evolution of outsourcing techniques and methodologies, we are certain that this book only makes a dent in the growing understanding of BPO. At the same time, there are timeless change and relationship management lessons in this book that apply to outsourcing and to global, interorganizational business relationships. We hope that readers will enjoy this book and that it provides executives with insights and concepts to make informed decisions and choices.

TOM DUENING

RICK CLICK

March 2005

Acknowledgments

W e want to thank the many individuals who contributed to this book. Among those who were instrumental in its genesis are the editors and writers we called upon for feedback and help on our prose. Most significant among this group is Mr. Doug Williams of Tomasini W2K in Houston, Texas. Doug's assistance in editing and condensing this material was both instrumental and timely. In addition, our Wiley editors Mr. Sheck Cho and Ms. Jennifer Hanley were very helpful and patient. Finally, we want to thank our families. My (TND) family put up with a lot of stress during the writing of this book as we moved from Texas to Arizona. My daughters Jennifer and Tiffany and my wife, Charlene, are my inspiration and foundation. My (RLC) move from Texas to California also occurred during the writing of this book and I thank my wife, Amy, for her patience during the process.

CHAPTER 1

The BPO Revolution

Overview

The Internet bubble bursts, and the world keeps turning. Terrorists attack the World Trade Center, and the world keeps turning. The global economy reels in the throes of a major recession, and the world keeps turning. Despite their unpredictable—and sometimes despicable—natures, humans are nothing if not innovators and perpetual optimists. In the face of doubt, ambiguity, and even terror, we continue to strive to build a better world. We are fortunate to be so resilient.

Even as our hopes for an easy peace and new economy prosperity in the twenty-first century were dashed within months of its arrival, we continue our pursuit. Part of that quest is based on the technological breakthroughs that seemed to appear with breathtaking speed in the 1990s. Standing on the shoulders of the innovators of the time, a new generation of visionaries has leaped ahead. Of all the vast array of novelties introduced in the past few years, none is more important than the creation of the global communications and information infrastructure that has now burrowed into nearly every city, village, hamlet, and encampment around the world. Fiber-optic cable spans oceans and continents. Low-earth-orbit satellites provide streaming images, data, and voice to the most remote locations. No place on earth, or in near-earth, is now beyond the reach of the information and data nervous system that was constructed over the past few decades. This *is* revolutionary, and this nearly universal telecommunications infrastructure is a major part of what gives life to the business innovation called *business process outsourcing*.

BPO Defined

Business process outsourcing (BPO) is defined simply as the movement of business processes from inside the organization to an external service provider. With the global telecommunications infrastructure now well established and consistently reliable, BPO initiatives often include shifting work to international providers. Five BPO international hot spots have emerged, although firms from many other countries specialize in various business processes and exporting services:

1. *India.* Engineering and technical
2. *China.* Manufacturing and technical
3. *Mexico.* Manufacturing
4. *United States.* Analysis and creative
5. *Philippines.* Administrative

Each of these countries has complex economies that span the range of business activities, but from a BPO perspective, they have comparative advantages in the specific functions cited.

A Strategy To Eliminate Noncore Functions

Because of the job shift that accompanies the quest to employ the highest-value talent, BPO has been both hailed and vilified. Business executives and owners praise it as a way to eliminate business processes that are not part of their organization's core competence. Back-office functions, such as payroll and benefits administration, customer service, call center, and technical support, are just a few of the processes that organizations of all sizes have been able to outsource to others who specialize in those areas. Removing these functions from their internal operations enables organizations to reduce payroll and other overhead. In an era when executives have been admonished by business commentators and analysts to focus on core competencies, BPO offers an opportunity to achieve that goal in a dramatic new way.

Like appliance manufacturers that moved production from the Midwest to Mexican *maquiladoras* or apparel firms that moved production to the Far East, businesses of all types and sizes are now shifting back-office jobs to international locations such as China, India, and the Philippines, where labor is inexpensive and highly skilled. In the past several years, companies have turned to these regions for increasingly sophisticated tasks such as financial analysis, software design, tax preparation, and even the creation of content-rich products (e.g., newsletters, PowerPoint presentations, and sales kits).

BPO Not Confined To Routine Jobs

With the increasing education levels around the world, BPO is no longer confined to routine manufacturing jobs or boiler-room telemarketing centers. Today's outsourcing involves complex work that requires extensive preparation and training. For example, Indian radiologists now analyze computed tomography (CT) scans and chest X-rays for American patients out of an office park in Bangalore. In the United States, radiologists are among the highest-paid medical specialists, often earning more than $300,000 per year to evaluate magnetic resonance imaging (MRI), CT scans, and X-rays. In Bangalore, radiologists work for less than half that. Not far from the radiology lab in Bangalore, Ernst & Young has 200 accountants processing U.S. tax returns. Starting pay for an American accountant ranges from $40,000 to $50,000; in Bangalore accountants are paid less than half that.[1]

Outsourcing of Service Jobs to Escalate

In the next 15 years, Forrester Research predicts that 3.3 million service jobs will move to countries such as India, Russia, China, and the Philippines (Exhibit 1.1). That is the equivalent of 7.5 percent of all jobs in the United States right now.[2]

Estimates from leading research firms more than support this trend. The Gartner Group, a Stamford, Connecticut-based research firm, predicts that:

- One in ten jobs at specialty information technology (IT) firms in the United States will move abroad by 2005, along with one in 20 IT jobs in general businesses—a loss of about 560,000 positions.

- BPO will reach $178 billion in revenues worldwide by 2005, representing a compound annual growth rate of 9.2 percent for the five-year forecast period.[3]

EXHIBIT 1.1

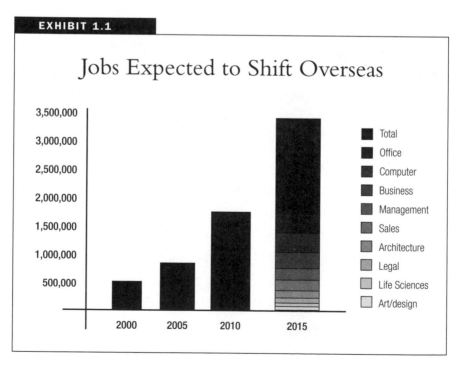

Jobs Expected to Shift Overseas

Additionally, market research firm IDC predicts that finance and accounting outsourcing will grow to nearly $65 billion by 2006, up from $36 billion in 2001. Two thirds of U.S. banks already outsource one or more functions.[4]

BPO has caught on as well with the venture capital community. In 2002, venture capital firms in North America poured nearly $3 billion into BPO firms and nearly $1 billion more by June 2003. Some BPO providers enjoy operating profit margins as high as 40 to 50 percent. Even though margins are expected to level out to between 20 and 25 percent as the market matures, these returns are greater than those being experienced in nearly any other industry.[5]

Concerns Over Job Losses

Despite this, BPO is not without its critics. There is no doubt that the history of outsourcing in manufacturing has been black-marked by the many Americans who lost their jobs and cannot find new ones in the traditional manufacturing sector. Today, everything from electronics to home furnishings is being produced by low-cost labor in places such as Shanghai and Monterrey. The prediction that free-trade agreements such as the North American Free Trade Agreement (NAFTA) would create a "giant sucking sound" as jobs moved to low-wage labor environments has rung true for many U.S. workers. Factories across the country, including many staples of America's industrial past, have gone silent— apparently for good.

Although such wrenching change is painful and unsettling, the resilience of the American worker to find new ways to create value in a global economy shows few limits. As the nineteenth century's Agrarian Age came to an end and workers moved from farms to factories, they adapted and built some of the greatest cities in the world. At the end of the twentieth century, the Industrial Age gave way to the Information Age, and many workers moved out of factory jobs into information-rich

IN THE REAL WORLD

Does BPO Increase the U.S. Unemployment Rate?

The Labor Department, in its numerous surveys of employers and employees, has never tried to calculate the number of jobs that are shifted overseas as a result of BPO. But the offshoring of work has become so noticeable that experts in the private sector are trying to quantify it. Initial estimates are that at least 15 percent of the 2.81 million jobs lost in America since the recession began have reappeared overseas. Productivity improvements at home account for the great bulk of the job loss. But the estimates suggest that work sent offshore has raised the U.S. unemployment rate by four tenths of a percentage point or more.

Among economists and researchers, one high-end job-loss estimate comes from Mark Zandi, chief economist at Economy.com, who calculates that 995,000 jobs have been lost overseas since the recession began in March 2001. That is 35 percent of the total decline in employment since then. Most of the loss is in manufacturing, but about 15 percent is among college-trained professionals.

Source: Adapted from Louis Uchitelle, "A Missing Statistic: U.S. Jobs that Went Overseas," *The New York Times* (October 5, 2003).

occupations and built some of the greatest technologies in the world. There is every reason to believe that BPO will help create a more tightly integrated business world that will lead to a more tightly integrated cultural and economic world. BPO has the potential to create new prosperity for workers everywhere through participation in a BPO-based business superculture that spans the globe.

Bpo: A Sociotechnical Innovation

Many executives and managers shy away from BPO because they wrongly believe it to be a technical innovation—one better left for the chief information officer (CIO) or other technology administrators. In part, this belief results from the IT origins of BPO. Many early adopters of outsourcing were those who needed software development expertise or who sought technical expertise to staff help desks and call centers. During the 1990s, the labor pool for such talent in the United States was tight, prompting many leading companies to search abroad for the personnel they needed. These organizations turned to international labor markets, where they were able to identify and hire highly skilled technical workers who were far cheaper than their U.S.-based counterparts. Today, the talent shortage in the United States has abated, but the cost savings to be gained by using outsourced talent remains.

BPO Transcends IT Origins

BPO has evolved far from these IT-specific roots and now encompasses nearly every business process. To be sure, the implementation of a BPO initiative will always involve a technology component, but for that matter so does implementation of a benefits administration office at the local beer distributor. The point is, nearly every modern business innovation comprises both a technical and a social component. Decision making, strategy setting, service delivery, and virtually every other business activity are now sociotechnical in nature, involving humans interfacing with technical systems. BPO is like that.

Fundamentally, then, BPO is a sociotechnical business innovation that provides a rich new source of competitive advantage. By sociotechnical we mean that BPO requires skillful management of people and technology (hardware and software). The manager who initiates a BPO strategy must find effective ways to introduce people to technology and vice versa. If left solely in the hands of technical specialists, a BPO initiative is likely to fail for lack of paying attention to the soft issues of human relationships, change management, and organizational culture. If left solely in the hands of nontechnical managers, it is likely to fail for unrealistic expectations about the potential and limitations of the enabling technologies.

Human Factors and Technology Issues

BPO is one of those interdisciplinary workplace innovations that demands a diverse set of skills to be successful. Initiating and implementing a BPO project requires a focus on several human factors, both within the organization initiating the project and within the outsourcing vendor. These factors cannot be ignored and must be handled correctly in order for the project to succeed. Human factors include:

- Developing various teams to manage the BPO initiative throughout its life cycle
- Reassuring staff of their role in the company
- Training people on the new way of doing business
- Dealing with job loss and/or reassignment
- Keeping morale high throughout the change process
- Encouraging people to participate in decision making
- Understanding cultural differences between the organization and BPO partner

The initiation and implementation of a BPO project also requires attention to technology issues such as:

- Compatibility of systems between the BPO buyer and vendor
- Data and system security
- Backup and recovery procedures in the case of system failure

- Data interface challenges and strategies
- Software and database compatibility challenges
- Data and knowledge management

These various issues will be discussed at some length in Chapter 6.

Driving Factors

Scholars who study how complex systems change over time are familiar with two types of change:

1. *Evolutionary*, which are changes a system is likely to produce based on its current design and goals
2. *Emergent*, which are system features or capabilities that would not have been predicted in advance based on the understood design and goals of the system.

BPO is revolutionary because it is such an emergent phenomenon and because there is no evidence that anyone set out to design the potential for organizations to use BPO. It grew from a set of driving factors, illustrated in Exhibit 1.2, that have unintentionally converged at this particular time to enable the shifting of work to its lowest-cost/highest-quality provider regardless of the provider's physical location. BPO is a business innovation that leverages these driving factors and applies them to practical business problems.

A discussion of each of these drivers follows.

Educational Attainment

The United States remains the global leader in higher education, but the rest of the world is catching up quickly. As more and more Ph.D.-qualified faculty return to their home countries with degrees from Harvard, MIT, Stanford, and other prestigious schools, they are helping to

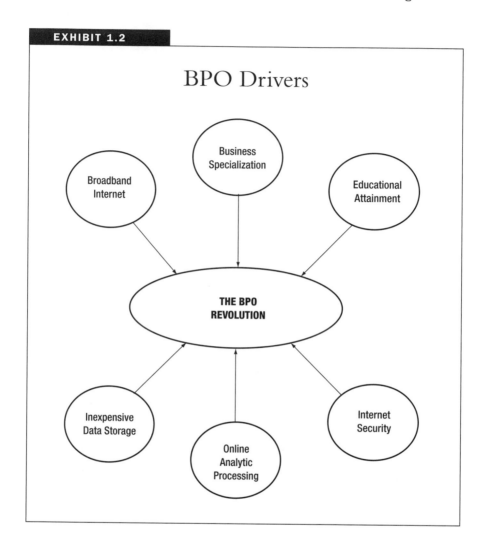

EXHIBIT 1.2

BPO Drivers

transform higher education worldwide. At the K–12 level, it has long been noted that the United States lags other countries, especially in technical areas such as math and science as measured by standardized test scores. The gap between the United States and many foreign nations has increased over time in technical education, which now also translates into fewer U.S. students seeking degrees in technical fields. In Asia, for example, far more students are pursuing science and engineering disciplines at the collegiate level than are their counterparts in the United States (Exhibit 1.3). Clearly,

EXHIBIT 1.3

Comparison of Asian and U.S. Technical Education

Bachelor's S&E Degrees in the United States and Selected Asian Countries and Economies by Field (1975–1988)

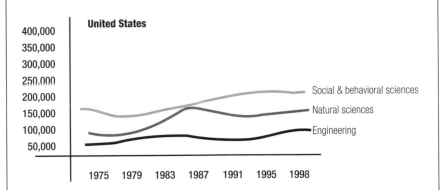

Natural sciences include physics, chemistry, astronomy, biology, earth, atmospheric, ocean, agricultural, as well as mathematics and computer science.

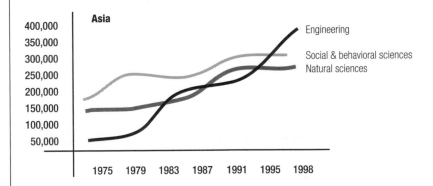

Asian countries and economies include: China, India, Japan, South Korea, and Taiwan. Data for China is included after 1983.

Source: Science and Engineering Indicators—2002.

they recognize that the business world increasingly appreciates and utilizes their new abilities.

Of the nearly 590,000 foreign students enrolled in U.S. higher education in 2002, more than 20 percent came from India or China. Ironically, the United States is not only relocating its coveted technical jobs to these foreign locations, but also preparing many of the workers who fill those jobs. The following list provides some sobering statistics on technical education worldwide that indicates why so many U.S. firms are looking abroad for the talent they need to be competitive:

- In 2001, 46 percent of Chinese students graduated with engineering degrees; in the United States, that number was 5 percent.

- Europe graduates three times as many engineering students as the United States; Asia graduates five times as many.

- In 2003, less than 2 percent of U.S. high school graduates went on to pursue an engineering degree.

- In 2001, almost 60 percent of those earning Ph.D.s in electrical engineering in the United States were foreign born.

- Among the more than 1.1 million seniors in the class of 2002 who took the ACT college entrance exam, fewer than 6 percent planned to study engineering, down from 9 percent in 1992.

- Less than 15 percent of U.S. students have the math and science prerequisites to participate in the new global high-tech economy.

- In the United States, more students are getting degrees in parks and recreation management than in electrical engineering.[6]

It now makes sense for U.S. firms to rely on foreign providers of highly skilled labor. The logic is simple: The quality of talent is high and the cost is low. Educational attainment around the world will drive BPO innovators to seek new ways to tap that talent. There is no way to put that genie back into the bottle. It would be foolhardy to the point of malfeasance for managers not to seek and use the best available talent that fits the organization's budget—wherever that talent may reside.

Broadband Internet

In fall 2003, *The Wall Street Journal* published its annual report on telecommunications. In the front-page article, the *Journal* writer stated, "After years of hype and false starts we can finally declare it: The Age of Broadband is here."[7] The article reports that by the end of 2003, 21 percent of all U.S. households will have broadband Internet, and that number increases to about 50 percent by 2008. It is also expected that more than 7 million businesses will have broadband connectivity in the United States by the end of 2003.

Broadband refers to the growing pipeline capacity of the Internet, allowing larger chunks of information to flow with fewer congestion issues. The term is generally applied to Internet connectivity speeds that are in the range of 2 megabits/second (2 million bits/second). Leading semiconductor maker Intel has predicted that by 2010 there will be 1.5 billion computers with broadband connections.[8] High-speed Internet access is becoming commonplace in regions where dial-up was once the only option. With broadband, workers in different countries can share data—an important factor in BPO—while consumers can surf the Web for the latest bargains.[9]

Growth in broadband connectivity is largest in regions where deployment is still scattered: Latin America (up 63 percent to 619,000); South and Southeast Asia (up 124 percent to 1.12 million); and the Middle East and Africa (up 123 percent to 107,000). The Asia-Pacific region is the runaway regional leader, with nearly 11 million digital subscriber line (DSL) users, followed by North America with 6.5 million and western Europe with 6.3 million. Eastern Europe has the lowest level of broadband connectivity, with barely 70,000 DSL users. In relatively mature markets, the percentage of DSL subscribers who use the service at home is much larger than in new markets and smaller economies, where businesses account for a larger percentage. In North America 22.6 percent of users are businesses, and the figure for Western Europe is 16.5 percent.[10] Hong Kong tops the world in broadband connectivity, with more than 66 percent of Internet users opting for the high-speed connection.[11] Exhibit 1.4 highlights broadband/DSL leaders around the world.

Broadband penetration is driven by the creative and business behaviors of users. Research from the Pew Internet & American Life Project, the results of which are shown in Exhibit 1.5, found a correlation between specific online behaviors and demand for high-speed access. Pew found that broadband users are extraordinarily active information gatherers, multimedia users, and content creators. Internet users with six

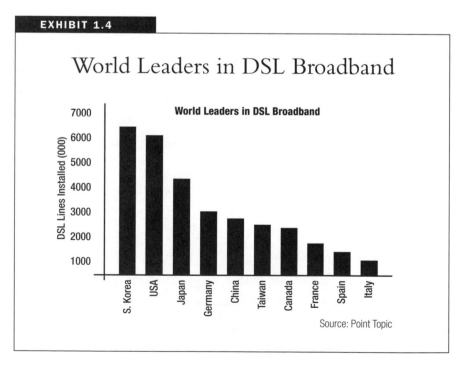

EXHIBIT 1.4

World Leaders in DSL Broadband

EXHIBIT 1.5

Online Behaviors and Demand for High-Speed Internet

	Broadband Users	Experienced Dial-up Users	Dial-up Users
News	41%	35%	23%
Research for Work	30%	30%	15%
Participation in Group	12%	11%	4%
Content Creation	11%	9%	3%
Stream Multimedia	21%	13%	7%
Download Music	13%	3%	3%

Source: Pew Internet and American Life Project.

or more years online who engage in similar activities are most likely to switch to high-speed access. In fact, Pew found that of those dial-up users who are contemplating broadband, 43 percent logged six or more years online, compared with 30 percent of those online for three years or less. Greater disparities in these behaviors are seen between less experienced dial-up users and those with broadband connections.[12]

Although Western Europe lags behind North America, by 2005 the European market will match North America for size. Undeveloped telecommunications infrastructure and economic volatility continue to hamper broadband growth in Latin America.[13]

Inexpensive Data Storage

One traditional danger of shifting work to a third party is the potential loss of organizational learning. When a process is executed internally, the organization's employees handle the related transactions and, over time, are able to discern and adapt to specific patterns or trends. Some of these patterns concern customer or competitor behaviors. When these transactions are no longer executed internally there is a potential for this vital learning to be lost.

But with the inexpensive, nearly infinite data storage space available today, this obstacle has been largely overcome. As file cabinets gave way to floppy disks, punch cards, magnetic tapes, disks, and CDs, storage has gone from scarcity to commodity. Technical advances have driven down costs, and a limitless cyberspace storage capacity now enables files to be retrieved whenever and wherever possible. Individual and organizational learning is literally a keystroke away.

This has enabled new ways of thinking about what is possible in the structure and procedures of the workplace. In times when storage was scarce, difficult decisions had to be made about what data to collect, keep, and eliminate. Even more limiting, decisions had to be made about who had access to critical information and when. In an era of storage overcapacity, however, an embarrassment of riches awaits savvy executives if they can move beyond the scarcity mindset.

Data protection and access controls must continue to play a role in a storage-rich environment, but they play a different role. In the storage-poor past, data access was controlled in part because storage limitations affected the number of copies of data that could be made. That barrier has been lifted by digitized document storage that allows literally infinite distribution of key documents, forms, and plans. In the past, gatekeepers, whose approval was needed to acquire and use company information, managed data access. That barrier has been lifted by precision software-based systems that enable rapid access to very specific data sets based on prearranged approval levels. These systems are constantly being upgraded to be more user friendly and can adapt quickly to unique work processes and systems.

With nearly infinite data storage, each transaction that occurs remotely can be stored for independent analysis. As is discussed next, sophisticated analytical software can then be used to mine the transactional data to reveal customer or competitor patterns—preserving and even enhancing organizational learning.

Analytic Software

Software is a major source of business competitiveness, as well as a major source of headaches for anyone who has ever booted a computer. Originally invented as a tool for us to work *with*, software has increasingly been designed to perform work *for* us. Expert systems, decision support systems, and artificial intelligence are all software tools that perform analytic tasks. Business analysis tasks were formerly the domain of human logicians, administrators, and executive decision makers. The advent of analytic software capable of recreating and possibly improving on human decision making has revolutionized the power of the desktop computer. Whereas the ideal of the Industrial Age was to eliminate the need for human thinking through mechanical design, the ideal of the Information Age seems to be to improve on human thinking through software design.

Online analytic processing (OLAP) has created a wide range of new possibilities in workplace structure, including effects on hiring practices, organizational design, and productivity. Although OLAP has enabled some human resources to be eliminated, it has also placed a premium on individuals who can use the sophisticated output and create new value with it.

Software that provides humanlike data output has opened the door to the possibility for data and information to seek lower-cost labor in the same way that manufacturing has done. Computational systems that have replaced human analysts range from trend analysis in sales and marketing to workflow optimization on the shop floor.

Before the advent of sophisticated OLAP software, it was necessary for highly educated people to analyze a firm's data and information to make it useful. In general, the more highly educated the labor, the more costly it is. As software replaces humans in an ever-widening array of business analysis functions, the roles left to people are increasingly confined to implementation tasks. The training required to implement the results of processed data is usually less extensive than that required to analyze it in the first place. Reliable data analysis software can eliminate high-cost analyst labor and replace it with relatively lower-cost implementation labor. For many business processes, the outcomes of processed data are predictable within a range. Business rules can be developed to specify the actions required within a range of possible outputs. In the case of an outlier, it is simple enough for the data implementation specialist simply to escalate the output to a few management-level analysts for additional processing.

Analysts traditionally have been the white-collar middle managers who served as the glue, gatekeepers, and information stewards in organizations of all sizes. The transition of analyst jobs from inside the organization to outsourcing partners will displace many of these middle-level roles in organizations. In fact, as the development of analytic software continues, it is likely that the swath of job shift in middle management will grow wider and reach ever-higher levels of the organization chart.

Internet Security

Internet security refers to the ability to send information and data (including voice) over the Internet without fear of leakage, espionage, or outright loss. It is critical for companies to be certain that their data integrity will be maintained despite its movement around the globe in the servers, routers, and computers that make up the World Wide Web.

In the past, many executives were reluctant to conduct any back-office business transactions over the Internet or beyond their own four walls because they felt the security risks outweighed the value proposition. However, in today's world of ever-changing technology advancements, most executives are more computer savvy and better understand the security protocols now available. With these new technical breakthroughs, companies can now work within virtual walls with the same level of security they enjoyed within physical walls.

One of the most significant enablers of this new virtual workspace is the use of Kerberos technology, developed at the Massachusetts Institute of Technology (MIT) as a cryptographic environment. This technology allows computer systems to use digital certificates for authentication within their transactions. Kerberos is just one piece of a much larger security framework now in place. Security systems today include proxy servers, passwords, authentication, firewalls, encryption layering, certificates, virtual private networks, open systems interconnection, and extranets. With these advances, two companies can partner and safely share resources in the virtual world.

In addition to the security innovations at the technical level, there have been significant changes at the policy and regulatory levels. Most organizations have enacted internal policies to protect sensitive data and information, including institution of security access to physical facilities and requirements for employees to wear identification badges. At the regulatory level, national governments have instituted laws regarding data security. For example, the Indian IT Act of 2000 addresses privacy-related issues and attempts to define *hacking* and *computer evidence*. It also strongly prescribes the implementation of digital signatures and public key infrastructure (PKI) for facilitating secure transactions. The data protection laws enacted by the United Kingdom and the European Union (EU) are considered to be benchmarks in international privacy laws.

Beyond that, several international certifications and standards mitigate security risks. Most BPO providers adhere to one or more of these standards and have received the appropriate certifications. Global and national compliance benchmarks include:

- *BS 7799.* First published in February 1995, BS 7799 is a comprehensive set of controls comprising best practices in information security. It is intended for use by organizations of all sizes and serves as a single reference point for identifying a range of controls needed for most situations where information systems are used in industry and commerce. It was significantly revised and improved in May 1999 and a year or so later published by the International Organization for Standardization (ISO).

- *ISO 17799.* This is an internationally recognized information security management standard that was first published in December 2000.

- *HIPAA.* The Health Insurance Portability and Accountability Act of 1996 (HIPAA) establishes standards for the secure electronic exchange of health data. Health care providers and insurers who transmit data electronically must comply with HIPAA security standards.

The new laws governing data protection, organizational policies, and new technologies have converged to create a highly secure—although

TIPS & TECHNIQUES

Three Security Prerequisites

There is little question that Internet security has increased dramatically in recent years. But organizations entering into a BPO arrangement should nonetheless undertake three essential tasks:

❶ Educate themselves on security best practices.

❷ Identify their own security needs and concerns.

❸ Thoroughly review all potential BPO vendors to ensure that they have the processes and capabilities in place to meet and exceed identified and anticipated security requirements.

still imperfect—communications infrastructure. Although hackproof systems have yet to be constructed, the ever-more-complex barriers erected to prevent cyberespionage and cybercrime make them increasingly less attractive projects for weekend hackers and an expensive undertaking for anyone else.

Business Specialization

Since the days of Adam Smith, capitalist economists have touted the benefits of specialization as a key to productive exchange among economic agents. The famous example of the pin factory used by Smith has stood the test of time. His eloquent analysis of the division of labor in the production of pins and the vastly greater output that would occur if people specialized in a part of the process can be applied to nearly any product or service.[14] As it turns out, in a world where business-to-business (B2B) services have become as common to the economy as business-to-consumer (B2C) products and services, the basic economic agent can as readily be construed to be a business firm as it could be a person.

Business specialization has been urged for several decades. Former General Electric CEO Jack Welch, for example, famously stated that GE must be No. 1 or 2 in the world in a given business or it should get out of that business. In their popular book *Competing for the Future*, C. K. Pralahad and Gary Hamel called on businesses to focus on their "core competency." They urged companies to develop a portfolio of core competencies around the customers they serve.[15]

The admonition to focus on core competence, if pursued logically, leads to the idea that a business organization should operate as few non-revenue-producing units as possible. In the early days of a business, when the firm is small and everyone pitches in to do whatever is necessary for the business to succeed, it is easy to call everything core. However, as a business grows, and as administration and overhead grow with it, there are many things a business does that are expensive but not directly involved in revenue generation. Accounting, legal counsel, payroll administration, human resources, and other processes are all necessary for the business to operate, but they are not tied directly to the top line of the income statement. If a business truly focused only on its core competence, it would not operate those units that do not directly affect serving customers and generating revenue.

This executive-level mind shift could easily be overlooked as a driving factor of the BPO revolution, but it is crucial. Transformational organizational changes—paradigm shifts, if you will—often cannot occur until a sufficient number of managers and executives have changed their thinking about the form and function of their organization. Such mind shifts can occur through education and experience, but they are far more likely to be a result of competitive pressures.

As B2B operations have flourished, the potential for firms to shed more and more of their noncore activities has accelerated. For example, it is estimated that 2 to 3 million Americans are coemployed in a professional employer organization (PEO) arrangement. PEOs operate in every state, and the industry continues to grow at an average of 20 percent each year. Today, it is estimated that about 800 PEO companies are responsible for generating more than $43 billion in gross revenues.[16] Many firms today have simply eliminated their personnel function by outsourcing their employees to a PEO.

The potential for B2B firms to exist and to provide the specific services they do is based entirely on their ability to add value to their clients' businesses. If these firms were unable to provide high-quality, lower-cost services, they would not exist. At the same time, they would not be in business without the relatively new concept of core competence driving management thinking and behavior. Just as quality and customer service seem to be patently correct ways to organize a business today, they have not always been important factors to business managers. Ford was an early adopter of quality management in the United States, but only because Japanese automakers had begun to erode its domestic market share. Until then, American automakers and manufacturers in general did not pay attention to quality as a major factor in their production processes.

Likewise, the idea of focusing—really focusing—on core competencies did not seem important and strategic until some organizations demonstrated that they actually are able to perform better by outsourcing their internal processes. Early BPO adopters among *Fortune* 100 companies include British Petroleum, IBM, American Express, AT&T, and General Electric. These pioneers were able to risk outsourcing noncore processes. In many cases they succeeded; sometimes they failed. But they blazed the BPO trail, and the lessons they learned along the way now ensure a higher probability of success for those firms that follow the leaders.

Bpo Types

BPO has usually been discussed in terms of the international relocation of jobs and workplace functions. In reality, there are three types of BPO: (1) offshore, (2) onshore, and (3) nearshore, and they differ in both location and function served (Exhibit 1.6). Organizations are prone to use any or all of these types, depending on their needs and the BPO initiative being implemented. In some cases, firms use a combination of types to achieve their objectives.

Offshore: Larger Challenge, Greater Reward

Offshore BPO is the most challenging type of this relatively new approach to conducting business, but it is also the most potentially rewarding. It began with movement of factory jobs overseas and has been made both famous and infamous with stories of suddenly prosperous geographic regions mixed with stories of exploitative labor practices. Yet despite the criticism leveled at some companies that outsource

EXHIBIT 1.6

BPO Types

Type	Location	Functions
Offshore	India	Manufacturing
	China	Programming
	Philippines	Financial Analysis
	Russia	Call Center
Nearshore	Mexico	Manufacturing
	Canada	Call Center
	Central America	
	Latin America	
Onshore	United States	HR Administration
		Call Center

processes and functions to international labor markets, the advantages of doing so continue to outweigh the disadvantages. By benefiting from lower wages overseas, U.S. managers can cut overall costs by 25 to 40 percent while building a more secure, more focused workforce in the United States.[17]

The complexity of business functions being moved offshore continues to increase. As such, organizations using the offshore approach have developed a variety of models to ensure continuity. Some have utilized a model known as *offshore insourcing,* in which the organization establishes a wholly owned subsidiary in the international market and hires local labor. An extension of this is the so-called build–operate–transfer (BOT) model. Organizations buy offshore companies specializing in a business process, operate them jointly for a year or so, and then transfer the firm to internal control (insource).

Two Giants Take the Offshore BPO Lead

GE Capital's International Services unit, which provides everything from risk calculation to IT services and actuarial analysis for GE worldwide, has grown from 634 employees to 17,000 during the past five years. More than half of those workers are in India, and they are not being used for mindless data entry. In India every employee has a college degree, and more than 1,200 have a master's degree in business administration (MBA).

Microsoft has about 200 employees developing software in Bangalore, where it opened its first non–U.S.-based product development center five years ago. In July 2003, the company announced it would shift more U.S.-based jobs to India as it seeks to lower technical support and development costs. Microsoft will increase its staff in India in the coming years, as the country continues to turn out tens of thousands of English-speaking engineers annually.

Sources: Adapted from Reed Stevenson and Anshuman Daga, "Microsoft Shifting Development, Support to India," Reuters News Service, July 2, 2003; and Nelson D. Schwartz, "Down and Out in White Collar America," *Fortune* (June 23, 2003): 82.

It is important to note that there is no one-size-fits-all approach to offshore BPO. With the growing list of companies outsourcing at least some business functions to offshore vendors, the range of possible approaches will grow as well. This makes it increasingly likely that the next adopter of offshore BPO will find a model suitable to its needs.

Onshore: Outsourcing to U.S.-Based Firms

It would be a mistake to see BPO as an international business phenomenon alone. Many U.S. companies are outsourcing back-office functions to American-based firms. A prominent example of this is payroll outsourcing, which is managed by several large U.S. companies. Automatic Data Processing (ADP) provides a range of payroll administration services, time sheets, and tax filing and reporting services. The firm has more than 40,000 employees and, as an indication perhaps of the future potential of the firm, has seen Warren Buffet steadily increasing his company's position in its stock.

There are many reasons a firm will use BPO. The cost savings that result from moving back-office processes to low-wage environments is the reason cited most often. However, firms can also use BPO to transfer service functions to best-in-class performers to gain competitive advantage. A firm that outsources customer service functions to a firm that specializes in and provides world-class support in that area will perform at a higher level in that function than its competitors. Moving to a best-in-class provider may actually increase costs in the short run in the interest of developing competitive advantage. Under this rationale, BPO is a strategic investment that is designed to upgrade service levels at a cost, with the intent of increasing revenues through enhanced competitiveness. What matters most is the acquisition of partners that provide market-shifting capabilities for the firm doing the outsourcing.

Many U.S.-based outsourcing firms use the world-class provider strategy to acquire business. Staked to a head start over their low-cost international rivals, U.S.-based outsourcing firms must continuously innovate and seek new ways to provide value to remain in front. They are worth considering for services, even if their costs are higher and strategic advantage is the goal of an organization's BPO initiative.

Nearshore: Outsourcing In North America

Nearshore outsourcing is a relatively new term that refers to the practice of outsourcing on the North American continent. International issues will arise when American firms outsource to Mexico, Canada, or Central

America, but they are likely to be less complex than those that attend outsourcing arrangements in, for example, India or China. Nearshore outsourcing allows companies to test the BPO waters without the level of risk associated with going offshore. Firms that go with a nearshore strategy are often seeking cost savings, but they are also occasionally able to find best-in-class providers of the services they need.

For example, Mortgage Electronic Registration Systems, an organization created by the mortgage banking industry to develop systems for mortgage tracking, is moving its customer relationship management (CRM) function from Michigan to Nova Scotia. The move is expected to save 15 percent annually on CRM costs. The company could have saved even more by outsourcing with firms in India, but it wanted to keep its CRM operations closer to home.

A Strategic Question: To BPO or Not to BPO?

BPO has managers around the world asking not only what it can do *for* them, but also what it might do *to* them. They are excited about the potential for BPO to help manage costs and improve their balance sheets. Under constant pressure from analysts to control head count, outsourcing back-office activities to contract laborers in remote corners of the world can provide welcome and quick relief. Whether the labor source is in India, Pakistan, China, or some other international port, the prevalence of high-speed Internet provides opportunities for real-time back-office support regardless of location.

At the same time, new questions are emerging and new challenges in organizational design and leadership are arising. Many organizational leaders remain skeptical about BPO because of the lingering aftereffects of the tech bubble burst. Their memories are still fresh with images of the "change the world" mentality of the tech bubble and its dismayingly rapid crash. The very thought of investing in new business models right now—especially those with a technology or Internet component—is very difficult for many managers and executives.

Many leaders are also concerned about the risks of BPO. They are unsure about the information security issues associated with outsourcing back-office processes. For example, in order for a BPO vendor to assist a client in managing employee benefits, the vendor must have access to some of the organization's most sensitive and mission-critical information. The thought of shipping this data overseas to be managed and used by individuals who are not bound by the organization's formal and informal controls is enough to keep a manager awake at night.

A Business Strategy—Not a Technology

BPO is based on the fundamental proposition that organizations should focus on what they do best and outsource everything else. If a company markets and sells sporting goods, it should spend substantially *all* of its time doing that and as little time as possible managing its accounting, customer service, and employee benefits plans. In theory, the concept makes a great deal of sense. In practice, it still seems to invite a new set of challenges that may cost more than the problems it is supposed to solve.

It is critical to point out that BPO is not a technology or a technology system; it is a business strategy. In that regard, to BPO or not to BPO is a question nearly anyone who manages a business process must now confront. As a strategic choice, the BPO option is a live one for anyone with a budget, limited resources, and decision rights over a business unit. For some managers, the decision may even involve the continued existence of their own departments and their jobs. No one is likely to decide to eliminate his or her own job, so managers must learn to understand how BPO may fit into their overall responsibilities and develop the skills to manage the BPO transition and maintain it once it is up and running.

Taking advantage of business process outsourcing will be a challenge for managers in all types of organizations and at all levels within those organizations. As we move into an age of greater accountability among organizational leaders, boards of directors, and others with fiduciary responsibility, it is imperative for those leaders to ask whether the firm could perform better by adopting new business models like BPO. Furthermore, as firms within an industry adopt BPO, others will be forced to consider it as the traditional cost structure of their industry comes under pressure.

The Revolution Is Here

The competitive and regulatory pressures that will compel managers to take a serious look at their BPO options are only beginning to be felt in some industries. But the revolution is upon us, and its will is relentless. Competitive forces that drive each industry to seek the most effective cost-control measures are irresistible, and no management or organizational structure will be able to hold off the BPO revolution. This means that adoption of BPO is virtually inevitable. Managers must prepare for the changes that are coming by understanding the factors that go into making a sound BPO decision.

In addition to the basic choice of whether to use BPO, a host of technological, business process, and HR issues follow in the wake of an affirmative decision. The technological issues range from the type of electronic infrastructure that will be required to communicate effectively with BPO partners to the integration of new technologies with legacy systems throughout the organization. These difficult issues require the skillful assembly and management of a team of diversely talented individuals. Because BPO is fundamentally a strategic issue, managers cannot simply call on their firm's CIO or systems administrators to decide how to achieve an outsourcing relationship. The web of relationships that make up successful BPO initiatives will be based on an array of managerial actions and skills that are unlikely to be present in any single manager or executive.

Summary

Business process outsourcing is the movement of functions from inside the organization to an outside service provider. It has been widely praised as a strategy for eliminating business processes that are not part of an organization's core competence, including back-office functions such as payroll and benefits administration, customer service, call center, and technical support. Despite its demonstrable bottom-line benefits, however, BPO has come under attack for eliminating jobs, often by moving them offshore to lower-cost, higher-value locations.

Yet the fact remains, BPO has emerged as a viable business strategy. Advances in technology, ranging from improved Internet security to inexpensive data storage, have combined with educational and business drivers to enable organizations to maximize the benefits of the BPO revolution. With multiple models offering varying degrees of challenge, and the likelihood that additional models will evolve, organizations have numerous options that can help secure their business objectives. There is no doubt that BPO is a virtual inevitability. As such, executives must determine if and how it can benefit their organizations, and how their organizations can and must prepare for the BPO revolution.

Endnotes

1. Nelson D. Schwartz, "Down and Out in White-Collar America," *Fortune* (June 23, 2003): 79–86.

2. William Spain and Andrea Coombes, "Worked Over: Job Exports Seen Constraining U.S. Recovery," *CBS Marketwatch* (August 29, 2003).

3. "Users of BPO Report High Satisfaction with Existing Relationships," Gartner, Inc. (October 7, 2002): 1.

4, Benjamin Beasley-Murray, "Business Process Outsourcing Gains Ground," *Global Finance* (September 2003): 54–56.

5. "BPO Profit Set to Shrink, Says IDC," *Computergram Weekly* (August 5, 2003): 7–8.

6. Texas Instruments, *www.ti.com/corp/docs/press/company/2003/c03033.shtml*.

7. Dennis K. Berman, "Profiting from the Broadband Revolution," *Wall Street Journal Reports: Telecommunications* (October 13, 2003): R1, R4.

8. Michael J. Miller, "Rejecting the Tech Doomsayers," *PC Magazine* (July 2002): 7.

9 Jodie Kirshner, "A Surge for Broadband," *U.S. News & World Report* (June 30, 2003): 17.

10. "DSL Subscribers Almost 26 Million Worldwide," *Computergram Weekly* (August 29, 2002).

11. Paris Lord, "SAR Tops Broadband Use Survey," *Hong Kong Imail* (August 16, 2002).

12. Robyn Greenspan, "Broadband Based on Behavior," *CyberAtlas* (May 19, 2003).

13. "Broadband Worldwide," *eMarketer,* 2003.

14. National Association of Professional Employer Organizations, *www.napeo.org*.

15. Gary Hamel and C.K. Prahalad, *Competing for the Future* (Cambridge, MA: Harvard Business School Press, 1996).

16. "Berkshire Discloses Larger ADP Holding," Reuters News Service, August 25, 2003.

17. Paul McDougall, "Offshore Outsourcing Moves into the Back Office," *Information Week* (July 14–21, 2003): 22.

CHAPTER 2

Identifying and Selecting the BPO Opportunity

After reading this chapter, you will be able to:

- Implement a process that will assist in identifying which business functions—if any—in your organizations are candidates for a BPO solution

- Establish a BPO Analysis Team

- Map your business functions and activities using a three-tier analytic structure

- Better define and understand the core competencies of your organization

- Recognize the eight function types of an organization, and apply the BPO Selection Matrix to determine their outsourcing potential

- Establish performance metrics before the BPO initiative is implemented, and assess critical factors such as timing, cost, deliverables, and risk

- Build a convincing business case for which functions and activities could benefit from outsourcing

BPO is not right for every company, nor is it right for every process in a given company. But its promise compels managers to seek out BPO opportunities and exploit them where possible. Regardless of whether your company has formal functional boundaries, it has processes that may be suitable for outsourcing to third-party providers.

BPO was pioneered primarily by large companies that were eager to reduce their costs and bloated payrolls. Today, many small to medium-sized enterprises (SMEs) have discovered BPO advantages that enable them to compete with the larger firms that have been using outsourcing for years. In 2001, for example, 75 percent of BPO users were firms with greater than $500 million in revenue. By 2002, that number had dropped to 64 percent.[1] What is indisputable is that any business that has grown to more than about $25 million in sales has begun to encounter growth-

IN THE REAL WORLD

SME Uses Outsourcing to Save on Health Care Costs

An exhibits design company in Illinois has 25 employees. To control costs, the firm had whittled down its health care coverage over a period of years. As a result, it had begun to struggle to attract and retain talented employees. In an effort to remedy the situation, the company outsourced its HR and benefits processes to a professional employer organization (PEO). By outsourcing to the PEO, the company now can offer a lower-deductible plan with better health care and dental coverage, while gaining the use of a professional claims manager. The firm was able to offer its employees these additional benefits while saving 40 percent overall on its health care costs.[a]

[a]"Small Business," *Money* (Fall 2003): 93.

related challenges in back-office processes that may be suitable for handing over to an outsourcing partner.

Without question, the decision to implement a BPO solution for any organization has far-reaching consequences and risks. At the same time, these implications should not lead to paralysis—there are too many possible benefits to fall into the trap of doing nothing. It is important for decision makers to recognize that undertaking a BPO initiative is a *strategic* action. With the increasing sophistication of BPO providers, the decision to outsource is no longer one of mere cost savings or headcount reduction; it is also one of performance enhancement in critical functional areas: Is your technical support team overwhelmed by customer inquiries? *Consider a BPO provider.* Is your new-product development cycle too slow? *Consider a BPO provider.* Is your accounts receivable department tardy in tracking down late payers? *Consider a BPO provider.* In each of these examples and many others, the choice of adopting a BPO solution is based on improving the company's performance in that process. In each case, performance enhancement may mean much more to the firm than simple cost reductions. Exhibit 2.1 highlights some of the reasons that decision makers have cited as grounds for implementing a BPO initiative.

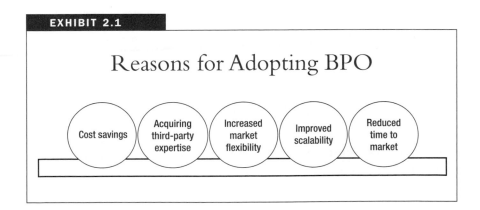

EXHIBIT 2.1

Reasons for Adopting BPO

Cost savings

Acquiring third-party expertise

Increased market flexibility

Improved scalability

Reduced time to market

A Process That Aligns Decision Making, Goals, and Needs

With these potential advantages, it is not difficult for organizations to justify a decision to at least investigate BPO opportunities. At the same time, inquiring into BPO has potential short-term organizational consequences that must be considered and addressed. The most effective way to analyze and select a BPO opportunity is through a six-step process that is deliberate, systematic, and minimizes risk. This process has been designed to integrate and align the decision-making process with long-term organizational strategic objectives and near-term organizational needs. If handled systematically, the BPO analysis and selection process can be an effective way for an organization to examine itself. Whether a decision to undertake a BPO initiative is made or not, this process will shine a light on organizational processes and activities. This illumination will, at a minimum, help the organization identify and change under-performing processes and activities.

A discussion of the BPO analysis and selection process follows shortly. However, it is important to first introduce a recommended team structure for exploring, initiating, and managing an outsourcing project.

BPO Project Team Structure

The value of using teams in the workplace has been elaborated at length by a number of scholars, consultants, and executive-authors. It needs no embellishment except to reiterate the sociotechnical nature of most outsourcing projects. That basic characteristic of outsourcing highlights the need for interdisciplinary skills to manage an outsourcing project effectively. Since such skills are rarely present in one individual, effective management of outsourcing projects will almost always require a team structure.

This structure begins with an executive-level BPO Steering Team, which is responsible for initiating the outsourcing project, communicating its links to corporate strategy, and seeing that project goals are being achieved. The Steering Team should consist of individuals representing the major functional lines of the organization, including finance, human resources, information technology (IT), and strategy. The recommended team structure for effective end-to-end BPO project management includes the BPO Analysis Team, the BPO Vendor Selection Team, and the BPO Project Management Team (Exhibit 2.2). The roles of each of these teams will be discussed in subsequent chapters.

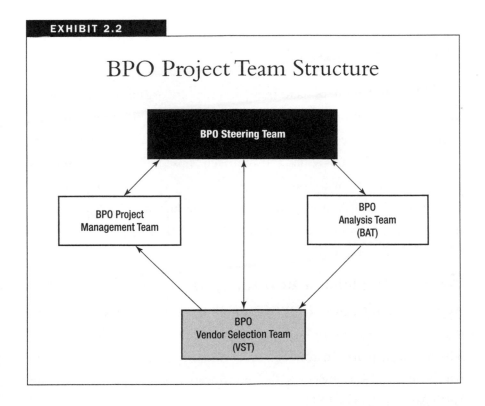

EXHIBIT 2.2

BPO Project Team Structure

BPO Steering Team

BPO Project
Management Team

BPO
Analysis Team
(BAT)

BPO
Vendor Selection Team
(VST)

Six-Step Process

Analyzing the BPO opportunity means identifying core competencies and determining the most effective way to support high performance in those activities. As many organizations have discovered, an increasingly effective way to support core competencies is by outsourcing noncore functions to third-party providers. By applying a six-step process to analyze and select BPO opportunities, organizations can better link BPO decision making to overall organizational strategy.

The six steps are:

1. Establish a BPO Analysis Team (BAT).
2. Conduct a current-state analysis.
3. Identify core and noncore activities.
4. Identify BPO opportunities.
5. Model the BPO project.
6. Develop and present the business case.

Although these steps seem transparent, many organizations overlook opportunities or misunderstand the true value versus risk proposition by skipping steps in the analysis. An organization can also find itself managing confusion if a non-systematic approach is used. This six-step process is not the only known approach to analyzing the BPO opportunity. However, it is a proven way to maximize the likelihood of success and minimize the risks associated with a BPO initiative.

Step 1: Establish a BPO Analysis Team

As discussed in Chapter 1, BPO is a sociotechnical business innovation that requires a variety of skills and expertise to be managed effectively. The multidisciplinary nature of a BPO initiative requires a multidisciplinary team to adequately assess the opportunity for the organization—the BPO Analysis Team (BAT).

IN THE REAL WORLD

AT&T Uses Team Approach to Outsource Its HR Function

When AT&T opted to outsource human resources, the telecommunications company signed a seven-year comprehensive outsourcing agreement with Aon Consulting. A team of functional experts in AT&T's human resource and finance departments orchestrated the outsourcing initiative. Each department challenged the other to prove the merits of the outsourcing strategy, resulting in a well-thought-out, appropriate, and cost-effective outsourcing initiative.

AT&T's finance and HR departments also developed an atypical process for determining which HR activities would be best served by outsourcing. Rather than ask respective managers to prove why their activity should be outsourced, the team asked them to provide evidence that their activity should continue to be retained in-house. In doing this, managers became more cognizant of the benefits of outsourcing, less adversarial and threatened by the strategy, and potential champions of it to the employee population. Ultimately, managers designated virtually every HR function for outsourcing.

Aon Consulting now provides AT&T with HR administrative, transaction, and payroll services—including the oversight of existing benefit plan providers—for AT&T's 70,000 U.S.-based employees.

The BAT should be chartered by the organization's top executive team, which will also serve as the Steering Team for the BPO project. It should consist of four to seven individuals who represent a range of organizational functions, including:

- IT
- Finance
- Human resources (HR)
- Strategy

Preparation and Training Are Vital

Preparation and training of the BAT is imperative to its success. Team members may be unaware of the potential benefits of BPO, so a crash course in BPO and its implications may be necessary. In addition to educating the BAT about BPO, the team must be knowledgeable about the organization's overall strategic intent. Because BPO is a strategic issue, the team must be prepared to build a business case for a recommended BPO initiative that is aligned with the strategic direction of the organization. Equally important, the BAT must be convinced that it has complete support from the executive team in its mission to identify and select internal business processes as outsourcing opportunities.

Establish Clear Goals

The formal charter offered to the BAT should include a clear statement of its objectives: to identify core and noncore business processes, to analyze which noncore processes may be good candidates for BPO, and to recommend whether to undertake a BPO initiative. Exhibit 2.3 provides an example of a BAT charter.

Developing the BAT will be much the same as developing other cross-functional work teams. Scholars have reminded managers that

TIPS & TECHNIQUES

Consider "Change Survivors" for BAT

When assembling a BPO Analysis Team, it is wise to include individuals who have shown an ability to adapt and change through previous organizational upheavals. These individuals may be important champions of the eventual BPO implementation and may be able to play a key role in minimizing resistance.

EXHIBIT 2.3

Charter XYZ, Inc.
BPO Opportunity Analysis Team

Purpose

To undertake a process of organizational discovery dedicated to determining if internal processes could be beneficially outsourced.

Goals

1. To identify, map, and classify core and noncore business processes.

2. To select which, if any, of these processes can be beneficially outsourced.

3. To prepare a model of the business costs and benefits of outsourcing identified internal processes.

4. To prepare and present a business case for specific BPO opportunities.

teams go through developmental stages, often defined as forming, storming, norming, and performing. Managers who charter the BAT must allow the team to develop interpersonal relationships and group norms. This can be facilitated through appropriate preparation and training. Occasionally, it may also be a good idea to provide the team with a training session on team dynamics and effective team performance. At any rate, savvy executives realize that the storming and norming phases are best managed using a hands-off approach as the team develops an identity and operating norms that will eventually lead to performing. Establishing a detailed charter and setting clear goals will help develop team independence yet keep it focused on results.

Step 2: Conduct a Current-State Analysis

The first performance task for the BAT to conduct is a current-state analysis, which refers to the exercise of examining, mapping, and categorizing internal business processes. Typically, this involves rolling up the sleeves and mapping business processes step by step on a white board or other erasable medium. The goal is to develop an understanding of how work flows within the organization. This can be difficult, requiring hard thinking and involving individuals from outside the BAT. But done correctly, a current-state analysis can unveil hidden bottlenecks and expose sloppy procedures that have become entrenched within the organization.

The Challenge of "Boundaryless" Organizations

At times the BAT may find that mapping the current business architecture is akin to trying to map geographic terrain—boundaries and borders are not always clear or obvious. A geographer standing in the northern Rockies would have a difficult time identifying the border between Canada and the United States. There is no line on the ground that conveniently divides one side from the other. Yet, the border *is* there, and it does divide clearly distinct political entities.

The situation is often the same in modern organizations. Over the past two decades, scholars and consultants have implored managers to break down barriers between departments and to create boundaryless organizations. This has tended to diminish the clarity of functional divisions within some organizations.

In their work on reengineering, Michael Hammer and James Champy asserted that most companies contain no more than 10 principal business processes.[2] However, in the book *The Process Edge*, Peter Keen identifies more than 100 processes that he refers to as "the process swamp" (Exhibit 2.4).[3]

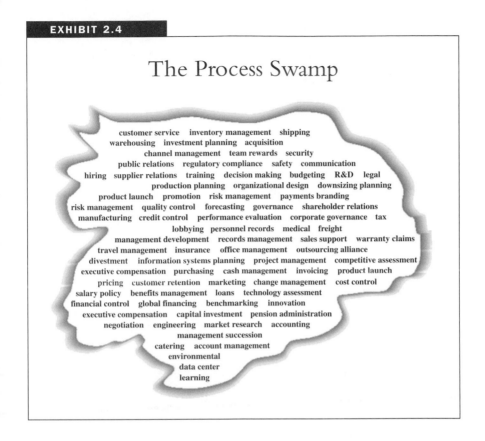

EXHIBIT 2.4

The Process Swamp

customer service   inventory management   shipping
warehousing   investment planning   acquisition
channel management   team rewards   security
public relations   regulatory compliance   safety   communication
hiring   supplier relations   training   decision making   budgeting   R&D   legal
production planning   organizational design   downsizing planning
product launch   promotion   risk management   payments branding
risk management   quality control   forecasting   governance   shareholder relations
manufacturing   credit control   performance evaluation   corporate governance   tax
lobbying   personnel records   medical   freight
management development   records management   sales support   warranty claims
travel management   insurance   office management   outsourcing alliance
divestment   information systems planning   project management   competitive assessment
executive compensation   purchasing   cash management   invoicing   product launch
pricing   customer retention   marketing   change management   cost control
salary policy   benefits management   loans   technology assessment
financial control   global financing   benchmarking   innovation
executive compensation   capital investment   pension administration
negotiation   engineering   market research   accounting
management succession
catering   account management
environmental
data center
learning

Determining How Things Really Get Done

The arrangement of processes within the organization constitutes its log-ical architecture. This logical architecture is often documented in the organizational chart, illustrating authority structure, reporting rela-tionships, and business units. However, understanding the firm's formal structure is only a surface feature of the logical architecture of the orga-nization. Underlying the organizational chart are the actual processes, activities, and behaviors that determine how things *really* get done.

The notion of an organizational process is similar to the concept of a system. Systems theorists have pointed out that the boundaries of a system are in part a function of the observer's point of view.[4] For example, the organization as a whole constitutes a system with its various inputs, outputs, and feedback mechanisms. Within the organization are other systems, which also have easily identifiable inputs, outputs, and feedback. The observer decides how to carve up the system into subsystems, usually based on practical concerns.

With this analogy in mind, the BAT should not be constrained to using the formal boundaries identified in the organization chart to identify work processes. Instead, it should use an approach similar to the systems theorists. The BAT should use a pragmatic approach to identifying organizational processes. That is, it should identify processes that produce meaningful results in the organization, not just those that are formally identified on the organization chart. One way to prime this mind shift is by developing a working knowledge of the types of processes BPO vendors are addressing. This knowledge will help the BAT identify similar processes within the organization. Beginning with a list of common processes in mind provides the BAT with a starting point for the next task, which is to develop a process map of the organization.

Using the Tools of Business Process Mapping

Business process mapping (BPM) has been used by organizations over the past decade as part of reengineering and continuous quality improvement. Many of the tools and steps used for those purposes can now be turned to analyzing the BPO opportunity.

BPM has been well documented and is routinely used by top firms to maintain a lean operation. Its objective is to define clearly the activities within a process and to identify activity owners. Identifying activity owners is critical because these individuals or groups can dramatically influence the effectiveness of the overall BPO project. Gaining their buy-in and support at this early juncture will ensure a more accurate process map and enable a smoother transition if the process is selected for a BPO initiative.

IN THE REAL WORLD

Soft Skills Required in BPO Leadership

Renee Baker-Arrington, one of A. T. Kearney's top recruiters of BPO project leaders, points out that successful BPO project leadership requires soft skills to work with people throughout the organization:

"There are a wide range of skills that companies are seeking today in executives and/or managers recruited to execute BPO projects. Among the most important skills is the ability to communicate. That term means a lot of things, including team-building skills, listening skills, political skills, and interpersonal skills. In addition, one skill that is very important to successful BPO projects—but one that is often overlooked—is empathy. Since BPO affects so many aspects of the organization, it's important for project leaders to be able to empathize with individuals as they adapt to change. Organizations have realized that BPO requires quite a few so-called soft skills to be managed effectively.

"Skills needed to lead a BPO project actually may differ depending on the project and the phase of the project. For example, the skill set that is necessary to develop and maintain the outsourcing vendor relationship is different from the skill set needed to identify and select a BPO opportunity. Managing the vendor relationship requires individuals skilled in negotiating, cross-cultural management, and controlling and measuring project outcomes. Often, the individual who led the BPO opportunity identification and selection process does not have the skills needed to manage it once it's underway.

"My hunch is that interest in hiring executives or managers with BPO project experience as a primary qualification is just beginning to grow. We seem to be at the beginning of a wave that could grow to significant size. As the implications of BPO are better understood and as more firms realize benefits of recruiting executives with BPO experience, I'm projecting a significant rise in demand for such experience. I also expect that there will soon be more formal education programs aimed at developing executive skill-sets in BPO. As I stated before, I think we are only at the beginning of the BPO revolution, and it might have a large impact on executive recruitment and hiring practices in the next few years."

A Three-Tier Mapping Approach

The business process map should be developed using a three-tier analytic structure (see Exhibit 2.5)

Tier 1 analyzes the process at the highest level, using the common business unit terms of the organization chart and linking these units into a logical structure. For example, the accounting department and the marketing department are Tier 1 process names.

Tier 2 features are the activities that occur within those departments to accomplish various tasks. These activities are often referred to as subprocesses. Many companies have discovered that while it may not be in their interest to outsource at the functional level, many *activities* within a *function* can be effectively outsourced.[6] Analyzing the structure and flow of activities within a function usually requires individuals working within the functional area to be involved in the mapping process. At this stage of the analysis, the BAT is seeking activity-level details that will help identify cost, productivity, and mission criticality.

Tier 3 refers to the process of identifying the resources that support the Tier 1 and Tier 2 processes—including HR. This is the part of the analysis where activity and function costs are identified, and where individual responsibility is linked one to one with the various activities.

The BAT should understand that it might be difficult to recruit individuals to help analyze organizational processes. If rumors of possible outsourcing are in the air, people may be reluctant to openly share information. To counteract this threat, the BAT should be encouraging about the opportunities of a BPO initiative—it does not necessarily mean that people will lose their jobs. Outsourcing often results in workers being hired by the third-party provider, as in an employee-leasing arrangement.

EXHIBIT 2.5

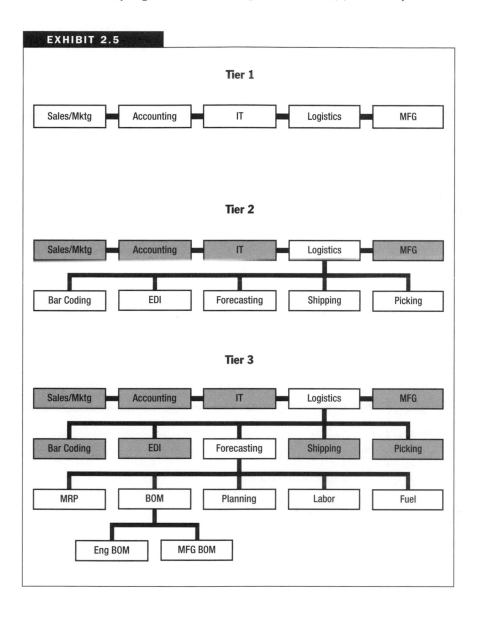

It also often leads to improved work processes and greater opportunities for higher-value work.

The BAT should also be aware that individuals brought into the mapping process might be skeptical about the intent of the analysis. Although it is not possible to provide complete reassurance that all jobs will be preserved, the BAT should work with the HR department to assure employees that their needs will be considered regardless of the outcome of the analysis. As counterintuitive as it may seem, it is possible for people to be willing to help restructure themselves out of a job if the appropriate support mechanisms are in place.[5] The challenges of managing internal change associated with the BPO initiative are discussed in greater detail in Chapter 5.

Step 3: Identify Core and Noncore Activities

Some consultants and business scholars have made identifying an organization's core business seem complicated. They offer example after example of organizations that have experienced decline in market share because they did not focus on their core competencies. Often, the prescription for returning to a healthy core competence is to engage in a series of high-level meetings that may involve scenario planning or other efforts to forecast the future and focus the organization on seizing competitive advantage. In reality, such meetings can be useful in setting strategy but are not helpful in identifying core competence.

Defining Core Competence

Other scholars have made identification of core competence far less complicated. For example, in his book *Managing on the Fault Line*, Geoffrey Moore said, "Any behavior that can raise your stock price is core, everything else is context."[6] Another simple definition is that core competence consists of "those capabilities that permit the firm to make the best response to market opportunities."[7] C. K. Pralahad and Gary Hamel were a bit more sophisticated, but they limited their definition of core competence to a process that exhibits three traits.[8]

1. It makes a contribution to perceived customer benefits.

2. It is difficult for competitors to imitate.

3. It can be leverage to a wide variety of markets.

Another widely held view, based on the so-called resource theory, holds that there are four elements of a firm's core competence.[9]

1. The resource is valuable.

2. The resource is rare.

3. The resource is difficult to imitate.

4. The resource is difficult to substitute.

A more applicable working definition is: A company's core competence is the process or processes that the front office, and especially the sales and marketing team, emphasizes to customers. This customer-centric conception suggests a way out of the endless debate about how to define the term. It seems obvious that an organization ought to be telling its customers what it believes it does better than its competitors. If it is telling them something else, either the message needs to be changed or the firm needs to focus on that something else.

This definition also distinguishes core competence from organizational strategy. Strategy defines how an organization defends, builds, and transforms its core competence over time. Deciding how to do *that* is a matter for scenario planning and forecasting—techniques usually practiced by upper management teams. The BAT must be careful not to get caught up in strategy discussions when the task in this step of the BPO opportunity analysis is to clarify and articulate the organization's core competence.

Once the organization's core competence has been identified, those processes that are noncore should also be identified and classified. Some of these processes will be more crucial in their support of the core competence than others. For example, if the organization's core competence is manufacturing, one crucial business activity may be logistics. This function may be more important to the support of the core competence than is, for example, payroll administration.

For the purposes of this discussion, there are three categories for business processes that remain within, but are not part of, an organization's core business: (1) critical, (2) key, and (3) support.

Critical Functions These functions are very important to a company's core business activity. In the example just cited, logistics is essential to the manufacturing firm. Critical functions must be performed nearly flawlessly and are potential candidates to become a future core competence if competitive conditions change. For example, a firm that excels in logistics to support manufacturing may one day eschew manufacturing and become a logistics firm.

Key Functions These functions are important to the organization's pursuit of its core business, but are not tightly coupled to the overall pursuit of excellence in the core business. For example, a firm's benefits administration function must perform well to create satisfied employees, but a perfect performance is usually not expected. Most employees, especially those on a fixed salary, will continue to function at high levels despite flawed performance in benefits administration. They may be annoyed or dissatisfied with a problem in their benefits program, but most will be tolerant and expect that the problem will be fixed to their satisfaction. A key function is one that people within the organization can readily identify, and they usually know who is responsible for it. Despite its relative proximity to the core, however, a key function is one that is unlikely ever to become the company's core competence.

Gulf Coast Refinery Outsources Non-Core Asset Management[10]

In 1998, a refinery and chemical plant on the Texas Gulf Coast determined that it was cost effective to outsource a portion of its asset management program related to corrosion prevention and life extension of buried, submerged, and embedded pipelines. After a thorough vendor selection process, the plant chose Corrpro Companies, Inc., to manage its assets. Services provided by Corrpro include:

- Monitoring and maintenance of cathodic protection systems on 198 tanks
- Monitoring and maintenance systems of waterfront facilities including docks and dolphins
- Testing and maintenance of 64 cathodic protection systems
- Bimonthly monitoring and complete annual inspection of corrosion protection systems using handheld computers
- Regular testing of 40 corrosion probes (data collected includes corrosion rates and temperature)
- Entering data in database and maintaining for risk analysis
- Evaluating data and identification of process excursions
- Performing condition assessment of protective coating systems
- Managing maintenance painting program

All of the preceding services are central to Corrpro's business model, which has enabled it to become skilled at analyzing abnormal conditions to mitigate equipment deterioration *before* problems occur. The economic benefits of outsourcing these activities accrue to the refining and chemical plant complex in several areas:

- Prevention of tank bottom leaks
- Prevention of piping failures
- Prevention of upsets that could impair operations
- Extension of interval between coating application

Corrpro has saved the plant over $3 million per year over the lifetime of the outsourcing contract.

Support Functions   These processes are essential to the operation of the business but will never become the organization's core competence. They are the most routine and fault tolerant of the three types, and include processes such as call center, payroll administration, and mailroom activities. In large organizations, most people do not know who processes their paychecks—and do not really care. They are aware when a paycheck is late, but they are also forgiving because they know they are under contract and will receive their check when the mistake has been corrected. Such functions are necessary for the organization to function effectively but constitute those elements often derided as bureaucracy or overhead.

Step 4: Identify BPO Opportunities

As business processes are identified and classified, the BAT begins to develop a feel for which processes may be candidates for BPO. This step requires that the BAT decide how the organization can use BPO to support the core competence in the current and projected competitive environment. In a highly competitive environment, where fast action is required, it may be necessary to consider outsourcing key and support functions immediately to a best-in-class provider in a winner-take-all strategy. However, in a less competitive environment, it may be prudent to take a more cautious approach to BPO, beginning only with support activities in measures designed to focus more on margin enhancement than on competitive positioning.

Factors to Consider

In selecting which business processes to outsource, multiple factors must be considered:

- Goals of the outsourcing initiative
- Ability to recruit a motivated internal project sponsor

- Business case supporting the initiative
- Timing of the project
- Culture of the unit slated for outsourcing
- Amount of work required to implement the outsourcing initiative
- Expectations of senior management
- Risk to business

The decision process involved in selecting which functions to outsource must necessarily be collaborative. Because BPO is a strategic choice for an organization, it must be determined if and how BPO fits into the overall strategy. This can be done only through broad, collaborative discussions at all levels and across all functional and process boundaries. Of course, no one gains if the BPO decision-making process gets bogged down endlessly in meetings and discussions. The general rule should be that, at minimum, people involved in functions potentially targeted for BPO should be included in discussions about the implications of outsourcing and the schedule to be followed.

These decision-making discussions will likely be difficult and will often include some levels of conflict. Managers in charge of facilitating these meetings can help them stay on track by reminding participants of the organization's mission and strategic plan. These guiding ideas and documents should underlie each conversation and should help drive the BPO selection process to a conclusion. That outcome is more likely to occur if clear and measurable goals have been established.

BPO Selection Matrix

Organizations can decide which functions or activities may be best suited for outsourcing by using a three-dimensional BPO Selection Matrix. This is a model of the three key factors, or dimensions, involved in evaluating a business process for outsourcing: (1) process costs, (2) process productivity, and (3) process mission criticality. There are eight primary function types that are candidates for outsourcing. (See Exhibit 2.6.)

Each type requires a unique approach and involves different factors to become a viable BPO selection. The BAT should place the various functions and processes examined in Step 2 at their appropriate location within the matrix. It is advisable that the BAT considers using the Tier 2 level of granularity in its distribution of processes within the matrix. Analyzing processes only at the Tier 1 or functional level creates the potential for many costly or inefficient activities to slip past the BPO analysis. Although some activities may be too tightly coupled to the process as a whole to allow them to be outsourced, their placement on the BPO Selection Matrix exposes their relative efficiency and

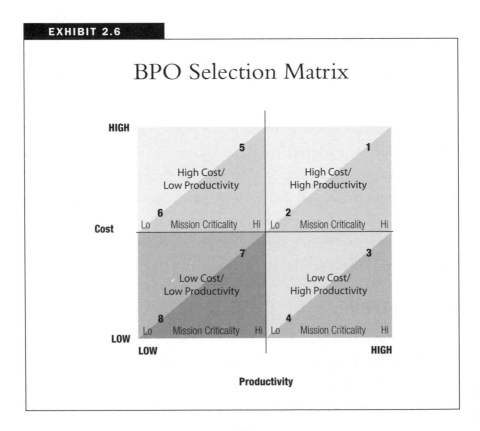

EXHIBIT 2.6

BPO Selection Matrix

effectiveness. This alone can be useful in making necessary changes to processes that are overly costly or unproductive.

The following list examines each functional type and the issues to consider when deciding whether the function or activity is a good outsourcing candidate:

Type 1. Those processes within the organization that are high on each of the three dimensions are difficult to outsource. The only factor that argues for outsourcing is the high cost. However, most organizations accept that highly productive labor that deals with mission-critical information is expensive. These functions are usually at the top of organizations, and often include C-level titles such as chief financial officer (CFO), chief information officer (CIO), or chief executive officer (CEO). This level is likely to be a last bastion of untouchability for management employees and will be the most difficult to address with an outsourcing solution.

Type 2. This encompasses all technical workers whose skills are highly valued and high priced, but who work on non–mission-critical systems. Such a process is a prime candidate for BPO. Individuals working in this type of process possess skills that have become more commonly available through lower-cost outsourcing alternatives. The major consideration in outsourcing this type of process is the high productivity demonstrated by the employees who comprise the function. The outsourcing decision must ensure that high productivity levels are maintained during and after the transition process.

Type 3. Type 3 processes are characterized by clerical employees who deal with mission-critical information. Their low cost makes them unattractive outsourcing candidates as long as productivity remains high. Reasons for outsourcing such processes are confined to the identification of BPO partners who can provide competitive advantages over the internal unit. In this instance, the decision to move forward with a BPO initiative would be primarily strategic. For example, if the outsourcing partner can provide market-shifting capabilities in the process area, it may be worth the effort to outsource the process.

Type 4. This type of process is a prime candidate for outsourcing even though it already has relatively low cost. The low productivity and low mission criticality of this type suggests there are few impediments to moving the function to an external provider. With labor costs in some offshore outsourcing relationships reaching levels as low as 20 percent of internal costs, it may be the case that outsourcing such processes not only increases productivity but also actually reduces the already low costs.

Type 5. Processes with high costs and low productivity are always good candidates for outsourcing. In this type, the process also has high mission criticality, making the outsourcing decision slightly more complicated. There are techniques for limiting a firm's risk exposure to outsourcing mission-critical functions. Choice of vendor becomes extremely important, as does the potential for backup and recovery. Fortunately, BPO vendors come in a wide range of capabilities and competencies. There are those that specialize in dealing with clerical-type activities and those that are familiar with and have built systems to deal with mission-critical functions.

TIPS & TECHNIQUES

Due Diligence When Outsourcing Mission-Critical Processes

Organizations should perform extensive due diligence on any outsourcing firm that will be handling mission-critical processes. This should include reference checks and, if possible, site visits. Additionally, top internal BPO champions should establish personal relationships with the executive team of the BPO provider.

Type 6. High cost and low productivity, combined with low mission criticality, makes this process type among the most likely to be outsourced. Technical workers who are in short supply in the United States, but who are in abundant supply in other regions, staff these types of processes. The greatest challenge to implementing BPO with processes of this type is that they are likely to be labor intensive and may result in large-scale employee displacement. Measures must be established to handle reassignments or layoffs in a manner that minimizes resistance to change.

Type 7. This process type is probably not worth considering for a BPO solution unless the company can identify a BPO provider that has strategically dominant services. Furthermore, the provider would have to ensure that the services are proprietary and protected to provide sustainable advantage. The only other time this process type should be considered is when competitors have established a strategically dominant position through an outsourcing partner and the organization is playing catch-up.

Type 8. Low-cost processes are always less-than-ideal candidates for outsourcing, unless they are also low in productivity and mission criticality. Such units are likely to be underperforming competitors, making them candidates for outsourcing to at least gain parity within the industry. Many organizations actually begin their investigation of the BPO opportunity by shedding Type 8 processes to outsourcing partners. This enables the organization to experiment with a low-risk process and work out any kinks that may exist in transferring data back and forth with the vendor. If BPO is in an organization's future, beginning with a Type 8 process may pave the way to a smoother rollout for more complex and risky processes down the road.

This BPO Selection Matrix provides additional insight into processes that may be outsourced for organizational advantage. The costs associated with a process will be explored as part of the Tier 3 analysis in Step 2. The productivity of a process should be assessed using standard industry benchmarks. If no metrics are available (which, unfortunately, is often the case), qualitative assessments and judgments can be used to categorize a process on the productivity scale. Finally, mission criticality is simply the identification of a process as critical, key, or support, as analyzed in Step 3.

Many business activities will not fit perfectly into one of the eight category types. For example, some activities are neither high nor low in productivity, but somewhere in the middle. In such cases, the activity should be categorized as low because it is likely that a third-party vendor could improve performance in the activity. In essence, if the organization is not performing at best-in-class levels in the activity or function—whether on a cost or a productivity basis—the activity or function should be classified as low. However, the three-way classification of mission criticality (critical, key, support) does have a middle ground, and most noncritical activities should be closely examined for outsourcing. Exhibit 2.7 is an example of a manufacturing firm's activities placed within the BPO Selection Matrix.

Step 5: Model the BPO Project

BPO is similar to any other strategic business initiative in that it is imperative to establish performance metrics before implementation. In the case of BPO, some of the metrics will be quantitative (hard) and others will be qualitative (soft). Hard data include such things as project costs, time involved, and opportunity costs. Soft data include employee displacement, effects on morale, and impact on community goodwill.

To establish appropriate performance metrics for a BPO initiative, it is critical to first establish project objectives. The BAT's charter charges it with defining the objectives of the initiative. Objectives should be identified both for the BPO initiative and for the transition process. At minimum, project objectives should include:

- Timing
- Costs

EXHIBIT 2.7

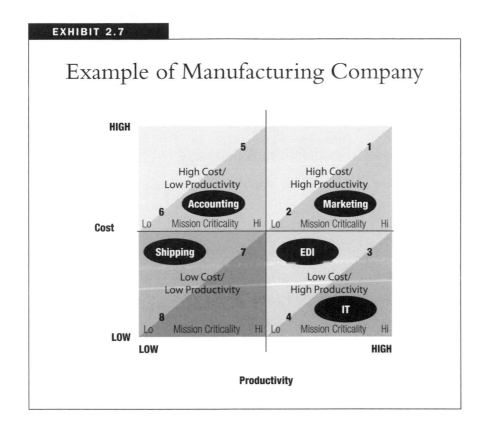

Example of Manufacturing Company

- Risk mitigation
- Deliverables

Timing: Keeping the BPO Process on Track

The timing of key events metrics will help identify whether the BPO initiative is on track during implementation. Event timing will include identifying realistic milestones for both the organization and its outsourcing partner. For example, developing a relationship with an HR outsourcing partner might involve shifting benefits administration and employee training responsibilities. For large firms this shift could be managed in phases, with each phase evaluated according to its time to implementation. At these critical deadlines, the project should be evaluated for effectiveness on a variety of measures. The metrics established by the BAT should include performance targets that are to be maintained once the BPO implementation is completed. These will establish the baseline standards that should be used in selecting a BPO partner.

Costs: Implementation, Transition, Maintenance

There will be costs involved with the BPO initiative, both cash and resource costs. The BAT should model the costs involved with both the BPO transition and with its ongoing maintenance. Implementation costs should be carefully detailed to include consulting or professional support required during the BPO analysis and implementation, personnel time, and opportunity costs involved with tying up key people during the transition. The organization should also monitor noncash costs involved in the BPO rollout, including resource costs, downtime costs, and risk mitigation costs. A more extensive discussion of the costs associated with a BPO opportunity is provided in Chapter 3.

Risk Mitigation: A Key Concern

Mitigating risks is a primary concern for a BPO initiative. Outsourcing necessarily entails ceding control of formerly internal processes, a prospect that is frightening to managers on many levels. Risks associated with outsourcing range from concerns over data security to a loss of organizational learning. Each specific risk can be mitigated, but there is no way to remove all risk from a BPO project. Thus, organizations need to weigh the risk of undertaking the project against the risk of not doing it. Risk mitigation tactics that should be modeled include provisions for what to do if the BPO provider fails outright. Having such contingencies in place will add to the complexity of the overall BPO project. Risks associated with BPO and mitigation tactics are discussed in greater detail in Chapter 7.

Outsourcing and Privacy Risks

The drive to develop better means of protecting the privacy of individuals has led to international innovations in data security. Although not yet perfect, these innovations should help reassure companies considering outsourcing projects that involve sharing of sensitive data.

A primary driver of information security is the need to protect medical records, resulting in the Health Insurance Portability and Accountability Act of 1996 (HIPAA). This act includes stringent data management standards to ensure that patient records are securely monitored and maintained. Nonetheless, medical transcription is a process that many hospitals, and even many transcription service providers, have elected to outsource. Today, medical records are being relayed around the world, and transcription is undertaken in places like Pakistan and India.

Although this might give some hospital administrators fits, it is possible that medical data are more securely managed through outsourcing than through in-house services. For example, if a hospital employee transcribes medical records, there is little recourse short of termination if the employee threatens to post the records on the Internet. However, a commercial provider that stands to go out of business if the records are improperly handled has a greater risk. Thus, the market-based governance of the third-party provider may be a more effective security management mechanism than organizational policies.

This principle holds true for data security and BPO in general. The digitization of corporate data has created security concerns in every industry. These concerns are real, whether work is done in-house or outsourced around the world. Organizations considering BPO should mitigate data security risks through effective contracts. They should also be aware of the power of market-based governance mechanisms. The more a BPO vendor stands to lose by being sloppy with data, the more likely the vendor is to be a practitioner of leading-edge means of protecting that data.

Deliverables: Managing Expectations

Finally, the BAT should also develop clear expectations for the ultimate results or deliverables to be achieved through a BPO initiative. Many BPO projects are initiated with a pilot effort before a full rollout. The expectations for the pilot will likely be less ambitious than those for the full implementation, but they should be rigorous enough to test what is likely to occur when the switch is finally thrown. Results that fall short of expectations should provide insight into where the problems lie and how to fix them. They should also be used in a Go/No-Go decision strategy. One of the few tendencies in social systems that can be predicted with accuracy is the phenomenon known as *escalation of commitment* or the *sunk-cost effect*.[11] This well-documented effect occurs as a result of the tendency for people to continue to invest in a project that is going poorly based on their past investment, rather than on forward-looking prospects. People tend to escalate their commitment to a project that is going poorly because they have already invested substantially in it and do not want to lose the investment. Organizations implementing a BPO initiative should be aware of and avoid this trap. They can do so by having clear Go/No-Go decision points established ahead of time.

Step 6: Develop and Present the Business Case

Once the BPO initiative has been modeled for timing, costs, risk mitigation, and deliverables, the BAT next must build a business case for those processes that could benefit from outsourcing. This will include direct recommendations on which, if any, business processes within the organization are suitable for outsourcing. A business case is a written document that presents the methodology and findings of the BAT.

The methodology section of the business case should include a review of the process the BAT used to reach its conclusions, including:

- The people who were consulted during the analysis phase
- The research documents reviewed, books read, conferences attended, and so on
- An overview of analytic tools applied to identify and select opportunities (e.g., process maps)
- Copies of any research instruments (surveys, etc.) used to gather original data
- Minutes of the BAT team meetings

Clear, Concise, Thorough

It is imperative to be concise in developing a business case, but the methodology should be clear about the thoroughness of the BAT's investigation. Often, top executives will fail to act on recommendations if they believe the findings are biased or likely to lead to internal bickering or resistance. The more involvement and thoroughness that can be demonstrated in the business case, the more likely it is that actions can swiftly and surely be considered and taken.

The findings section of the business case should include copies of the process maps developed by the BAT showing the three tiers of analysis. Process gaps and inefficiencies should be highlighted. In the end, if decision makers elect not to undertake a BPO initiative, the process maps developed by the BAT can at least assist the firm in reengineering processes that have serious gaps and/or inefficiencies.

The business case should also include the business model for each process recommended for outsourcing. The model will summarize the costs, timing, and deliverables associated with each process. Detailed transition models should be kept on reserve for those decision makers who wish to have more information.

Finally, the business case should make explicit the goals of outsourcing for each process. The goal may be to reduce operating costs, but it may also include the opportunity to develop world-class capability in a critical process, to reduce cycle times, or simply to free up business resources for other applications. Whatever the reason, the business case should clearly state the goals of outsourcing for each process and the likely improvements that may be attained through a BPO provider.

Summary

The six-step approach to analyzing the BPO opportunity provides a systematic framework for decision making. The importance of developing and managing a cross-functional BPO Analysis Team (BAT) cannot be overstated. An effective and committed BAT will be the focal point for BPO-based organizational change, including internal challenges to the BPO analysis process. Team members must be carefully chosen for their commitment to organizational strategy, their ability to deal with and manage change, and their capability to communicate and work with persons from a range of disciplinary backgrounds. Implementing the decision-making process and developing a business case should be done deliberately, with attention to deadlines and resource constraints. Although the proposed systematic process is not foolproof, it is likely to help the organization identify inefficient or unproductive business processes, some of which can be outsourced and others of which can simply be fixed.

Endnotes

1. "Survey: BPO Moves to Small Business," *Silicon Valley/San Jose Business Journal* (April 2003).

2. Michael Hammer and James Champy, *Reengineering the Corporation: A Manifesto for Business Revolution* (New York: Harper Business, 1993).

3. G.W. Keen, *The Process Edge: Creating Value Where it Counts* (Cambridge, MA: Harvard Business School Press, 1997).

4. See for example, Ludwig von Bertalanffy, *General System Theory* (New York: George Braziller, 1968); or Stafford Beer, *The Heart of Enterprise* (New York: John Wiley & Sons, 1979).

5. Joann S. Lublin, "What Kind of Managers Target Their Own Jobs In a Restructuring?" *Wall Street Journal* (October 7, 2003): B1.

6. Geoffrey Moore, *Managing on the Fault Line* (New York: Harper-Business, 2002).

7. Bruce Kogut and Nalin Kulatilaka, "Capabilities as Real Options," *Organization Science* (November–December 2001): 744–758.

8. C.K. Prahalad and G. Hamel, "The Core Competence of the Corporation," *Harvard Business Review* (May/June 1990): 79–91.

9. J. Barney, "Firm Resources and Sustained Competitive Advantage," *Journal of Management* 17 (1991): 99–120; K. Conner, "A Historical Comparison of Resources-Based Theory and Five Schools of Thought within Industrial Organization Economics: Do We Have a New Theory of the Firm?" *Journal of Management* 17 (1991): 121–154.

10. From a personal interview with David Kroon, executive vice president and chief engineer, Corrpro Companies, Inc., Houston, Texas.

11. Barry M. Staw, "The Escalation of Commitment to a Course of Action," *Academy of Management Review* (October 1981): 569–576.

CHAPTER 3

Identifying and Managing the Costs of BPO

 After reading this chapter, you will be able to:

- Better understand the full range of costs, financial as well as strategic, that are inherent to a BPO initiative

- Apply a total cost management (TCM) model to BPO that helps identify both obvious and hidden costs

- Recognize and calculate the costs related to analysis, implementation, transition, and maintenance of a BPO initiative, as well as techniques and strategies that can mitigate those costs

- Determine whether it is in the organization's best interest to manage the BPO initiative internally or externally

- Develop a sound, strategic process for developing requests for proposals (RFPs) for BPO vendors, for reviewing proposals, and for selecting the appropriate partner

- Manage the often complex relationship between buyers and vendors in the BPO process

- Anticipate, adjust, and map BPO costs throughout the project

Make or buy? That is the fundamental decision that faces all organizations considering their alternatives for managing a business process. The decision involves many factors, not the least of which is the cost associated with developing internal capabilities (making) or outsourcing them to an external provider (buying). As illustrated in the BPO Selection Matrix (Exhibit 2.8), cost is one of the three primary elements of the BPO decision, along with productivity and mission criticality. Each must be weighed when analyzing BPO opportunities.

In a perfect world, where all other things are equal, the decision to undertake a BPO initiative would be based purely on cost-of-labor arbitrage—firms would simply source business processes to the lowest-cost labor, wherever it may be. But this is not a perfect world, and the various costs associated with a BPO initiative are not always easy to identify or forecast. The savings that are most often associated with BPO stem from the elimination of overhead, including jobs, capital assets, and real estate. However, the true costs involve far more than head count and capital investments.

Identifying and assessing the costs related to a BPO initiative are essential to the outsourcing decision and can help organizations budget appropriately. There are two primary areas of concern:

1. *Financial costs.* Hard costs associated with activities that must be undertaken to assess, launch, and maintain a BPO project.
2. *Strategic costs.* Soft costs that are difficult to quantify but can profoundly affect the firm's ability to compete.

While financial costs are often self-evident, strategic costs may not be so clear. For example, one strategic cost of outsourcing that is often cited is loss of organizational learning in the outsourced activity. This can lead to strategic blunders if the outsourced activity is important to the organization's core competence and the organization is not working closely enough with its vendor in a mutual exchange of knowledge. Strategic benefits can arise from a deep partnership arrangement between BPO buyer and vendor. Such a relationship focuses not just on cost-effective performance on the outsourced activity, but also on knowledge sharing, innovation, and reciprocal exchange across business processes, including the outsourcer's core competence.

Total Cost Management

The total costs associated with BPO cannot be forecast precisely. However, organizations seeking to undertake BPO can lessen the potential for expensive surprises by using an approach called total cost management (TCM). In the context of a BPO initiative, it refers to the process of identifying and developing a strategy for managing the costs associated with initiating and managing a BPO project.[1]

Exhibit 3.1 provides a high-level view of what is called the *BPO Project Life Cycle*. Each phase of the life cycle has multiple costs associated with it, some obvious and directly attributable to the project and others hidden and less easily attributed. For example, the BPO Analysis Team (BAT) will often require that non-BAT employees assist with the business-process mapping task. This means the employees will be pulled away from their normal jobs, if only briefly. Although it may be possible to attribute time-away costs to the BPO project, it is more difficult to attribute costs associated with disruptions in the work unit from which the employees came—disruptions that can linger long after the individuals assisting the BAT have returned to their jobs. Questions about the security of their

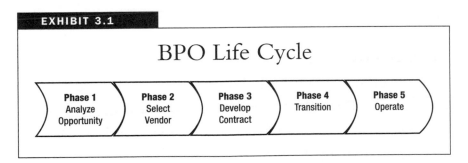

EXHIBIT 3.1

BPO Life Cycle

| Phase 1 Analyze Opportunity | Phase 2 Select Vendor | Phase 3 Develop Contract | Phase 4 Transition | Phase 5 Operate |

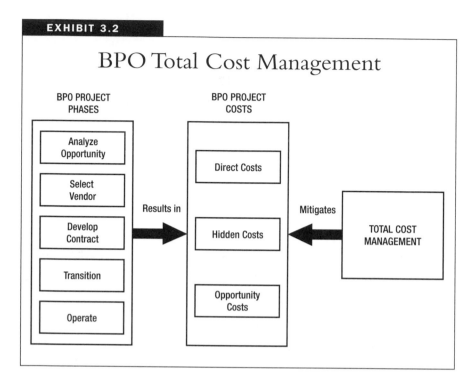

EXHIBIT 3.2

BPO Total Cost Management

BPO PROJECT
PHASES

BPO PROJECT
COSTS

Analyze
Opportunity

Select
Vendor

Develop
Contract

Transition

Operate

Direct Costs

Hidden Costs

Opportunity
Costs

Results in

Mitigates

TOTAL COST
MANAGEMENT

jobs, doubts about the intentions of the BAT, and work-time rumor exchange all sap productivity from the work team. These hidden costs are associated with the analysis phase of the BPO project. Using a TCM approach, these costs are identified, estimated, and attributed to the project.

TCM involves the overt or direct costs that can be linked to the BPO project, hidden costs that are quantifiable but less easy to identify, and opportunity costs that are nonquantifiable but capable of being identified and estimated. Exhibit 3.2 shows a BPO project TCM model that includes these varieties of cost categories.

Financial Costs

The financial costs associated with BPO are ongoing, as long as the project is active. Each project phase has predictable costs that can be forecast, budgeted, monitored, and mitigated. Additionally, each BPO initiative has a variety of less obvious yet insidious hidden costs. BPO project managers should include these in their analyses because many initiatives accumulate unanticipated costs that can threaten projects—and careers.

Analysis Phase Costs

The first direct cost to consider in the BPO analysis phase is associated with the internal staff that will be enlisted to conduct the assessment. As discussed in Chapter 2, organizations should use a team approach to identify and select BPO opportunities. Organizing a BAT means employees from diverse units will take time away from their normal duties to serve on the team. The time spent away from these duties is a direct cost.

Costs associated with removing individuals from their regular jobs can be calculated in several ways. One is to count the hours spent on the BPO analysis for each BAT member (and anyone else brought in on a

TIPS & TECHNIQUES

Capturing Hidden Hours

Regardless of how effective a time-capture technique is, it may not tell the entire story. For example, it is inevitable that BAT members will spend hours outside of their formal meetings thinking about BPO, analyzing opportunities in their minds, and talking with others informally about what the BAT is doing and learning. These extra hours are usually not calculated and attributed to the project.

One approach for capturing this hidden cost is to apply a standard multiplier to the hours that are logged as officially attributable to the BPO project. For example, a person may spend one hour outside formal meetings working on the BPO project for every two hours spent in formal meetings. A multiplier of 1.5 would reflect that informal project time and provide a more realistic estimate of actual costs.

In general, a multiplier between 1.0 and 2.0 is appropriate in estimating BAT member time spent on the BPO project during the analysis phase.

EXHIBIT 3.3

Task–Based Cost Estimating Model

Assumptions:

HR director day rate cost	$600
Material day rate cost	$150

Information from Project Plan:

Task start date	10/1/04
Task finish date	10/9/04

Computations:

Task duration (days)	9

Outputs:

Total personnel cost	$5,400
Total materials cost	$1,350

Total Project Cost:	**$6,750**

transitory basis) and multiply this figure by the hourly wage for that individual. The result of this calculation is then attributed to the BPO project. This approach is often referred to as *transfer pricing.* Project managers also commonly use what is called a task-based costing estimate to forecast personnel costs associated with a project[2] (Exhibit 3.3).

Cost of Third-Party Support

Another direct cost associated with the BPO analysis phase involves third-party professional support that may be required to assist the team. BPO consultants, market research specialists, and change-management consultants are just some of the outside professionals the BAT may want to consider utilizing. This cost can be estimated at the beginning of the project using several indicators, including:

- Prior BPO knowledge among BAT members and the organization as a whole
- Organizational history with BPO, reengineering, or other transformational change programs
- Top management support for BPO in the organization

BAT member knowledge of BPO is a factor because lack of such background will usually require investment in outside support. It is simply unrealistic to expect individuals with no BPO knowledge or experience to be effective BAT members. Thus, training and preparation costs should be estimated. A good rule-of-thumb estimate is to assume one week of person-time for each BAT member to read, review, and discuss what BPO is and how it can be utilized by the organization.

Organizational history with major change programs can also reduce BPO analysis costs. Firms that have such a history, whether with reengineering, total quality management (TQM), or something else, will likely be better suited for the self-examination process that is required for effective BAT performance. A history with transformational change, especially if the experience was positive, can ease the burden of the analysis process. Individuals throughout the firm will be more willing to cooperate and work hard to analyze BPO opportunities if they believe the process will result in positive changes. Estimating the costs associated with a lack of history in transformational change will be subjective. In general, the analysis-phase cost estimates should include an extra week of BAT member time if the organization has no history with transformational change.

Top management support is critical to the success of any organizational transformation. BAT members must perceive that they are empowered to dedicate their time to the analysis process. If top managers badger them about time spent away from their central duties, team members will feel conflicted and the BPO analysis process will likely take longer and be less effective. Top managers must clear the space necessary for BAT members to do their analysis, while maintaining reasonable expectations about performance in their regular duties.

Value of Learning from Consultants

Hidden costs associated with the BPO analysis phase include those that arise from a lack of organizational capability to analyze the BPO opportunity. Reliance on third-party consultants to assist with the BPO analysis is common and in many cases recommended. However, overreliance on consultants can lead to additional project costs throughout the implementation, transition, and maintenance phases of the BPO initiative. To avoid these hidden costs, BAT members and others should learn as much as possible from the third-party professionals. Failure to concentrate on organizational learning and on building a knowledge base for managing BPO projects will inevitably lead to additional costs. Thus, the organization should seek to develop internal BPO champions who will be responsible for absorbing, analyzing, communicating, and documenting knowledge gained from third parties and through the BAT's internal research process.

Mitigating Analysis-Phase Costs

Costs associated with the BPO analysis phase can be mitigated through a variety of tactics. For example, the exercise of mapping organizational processes in the interest of determining their suitability for BPO also reveals opportunities for reengineering. Processes that have gone unexamined over time almost assuredly have become bloated and inefficient in both subtle and not-so-subtle ways. The process maps developed during the analysis phase should be used to catalyze reengineering efforts directed at those inefficient or unproductive processes that are not outsourced. The organization will derive benefits from the analysis phase if it is prepared to use its findings for organizational improvement regardless of whether a BPO project is initiated. The organizational learning that is a consequence of process mapping is not confined to BAT members. As stated in Chapter 2, the BAT should invite individuals working within processes to assist with the mapping. These individuals can be encouraged to initiate changes to process inefficiencies when they return to their work units.

Another cost mitigation tactic includes the potential for a general improvement in work productivity as a natural result of organizational self-examination. The phenomenon of increased performance as a result of being observed is commonly referred to as the Hawthorne effect.[3] The reference is to the famous studies conducted between 1924 and 1932 at the Hawthorne plant of Western Electric, where employee performance increased merely because of the presence of the researchers.[4] Organizations can encourage operating performance improvement during the course of the BPO analysis based on this effect. Communicating the process improvement objectives of the analysis phase to everyone in the units under scrutiny can circumvent the potential for fear-induced performance declines. Getting people involved in the change effort is a classic technique to mitigate the hidden costs associated with the common human tendency to resist change.

Implementation-Phase Costs

The result of the analysis phase is a decision about implementing a BPO initiative. Implementation has several subphases associated with it, including:

- Identifying a suitable outsourcing vendor/partner
- Negotiating a contract
- Establishing a project map for the transition

Identifying a Vendor/Partner

One of the first decisions any organization must make after identifying a BPO opportunity is whether to hire a third-party intermediary to assist with the implementation. The decision is important. Obviously, conducting the implementation phase in-house can reduce costs in the short run but may add costs in the long run. Especially for large and complex outsourcing initiatives, the implementation phase can be time consuming and highly detailed. Third-party intermediaries that specialize in request for proposal (RFP) drafting, distribution, and response evaluation can reduce the time it takes to identify a suitable outsourcing vendor and allow internal staff to stay focused on internal issues associated with the pending BPO transition.

For companies that decide to manage the BPO implementation phase in-house, financial costs will include the time spent in crafting an RFP, distributing it to vendors, managing and responding to queries, and evaluating proposals. No RFP has ever been immune from questions from potential responders. And the international distribution of many RFPs raises the likelihood of misunderstandings and requests for clarification. Staff time will be needed to field questions—regardless of their legitimacy—from all over the world. A fair response process that limits the potential for liability requires each inquiry to be managed with equal care and interest.

A Months-Long Process

Depending on the complexity of the BPO project, it could take anywhere from one to several months to write a comprehensive RFP—one that articulates the scope of the initiative, the expectations for service delivery, the qualifications of the outsourcing firm, and the range of services that will be needed to fully outsource the process. On the vendor side, responding to the RFP can also be time consuming and labor inten-

When Low Costs Can Lead to Higher Costs

If an organization is merely seeking the low-cost provider for its BPO initiative, the selection process may (emphasize *may*) be made easier. However, that approach carries some risk. For example, a vendor that submits the low-cost solution may have scrimped on certain critical services or suggested reduced service levels. Evaluating proposals on price alone may in fact lead to higher costs later.

sive. As such, the responder may require additional information and clarification throughout the response period. The response phase of the RFP process may take another one to three months.

All told, it may require from two to six months or longer to complete the RFP process. Of course, at the end of that process the initiating organization has an inbox full of complex and comprehensive proposals, each of which must be examined to identify potential vendors that are best suited to carry out the BPO initiative. For many outsourcing RFPs, there may be up to 50 proposals from qualified vendors.

Evaluating RFP Responses

The process of evaluating proposals from potential vendors can take a month or more. Typically, this process moves from scrutinizing the written proposals to actual meetings with the leadership teams of the top two or three candidates, including site visits to their facilities. These meetings can add another month to the selection process because some vendor facilities may be in faraway corners of the world.

Organizations that manage the RFP process in-house should assume that proposal review can take from three to six months, depending on the complexity, scope, and range of services requested. They should also assume that the process will occupy 50 percent or more of the work time for one to two management-level individuals. Thus, estimating the cost of in-house management of the RFP process begins with the cost of one half to one person-year of management-level personnel.

The cost estimate does not end there, however. The decision to in-source the RFP process carries hidden costs. No matter how experienced the individuals managing the RFP process may be, going it alone likely means additional costs associated with writing an incomplete RFP, establishing an ineffective response-management plan, and selecting a less-than-optimal vendor. Each of these is a reflection of the fact that RFP writing, distribution, and management is not part of the initiating organization's core competence. This hidden cost can be estimated based on the relative experience of the project's lead individual(s). An inexperienced project leader could double the costs of the implementation phase compared to the cost of using a professional service provider. A highly experienced leader may increase costs by far less, but such a person probably commands a far higher salary.

Developing the Contract

The implementation phase of the BPO project will also have costs associated with negotiating a contract with the vendor and establishing a project map for the transition phase. It is highly recommended that the BPO buyer work with an experienced legal team when developing the contract. There is simply too much at stake in the specification of services, deliverables, and remedies to cut costs in this area. Although BPO contracting is discussed in depth in Chapter 4, organizations should consider this rule of thumb for estimating costs: In terms of internal time and legal review, contracting costs should be less than 5 percent of the size of the outsourced project. Thus, a $1 million project may have contract development costs of up to $50,000.

How GE Real Estate Manages Offshore Vendors

Realizing cost savings from offshore outsourcing often takes years of effort and a huge up-front investment. For many companies, it simply may not be worth it. "Someone working for $10,000 a year in Hyderabad can end up costing an American company four to eight times that amount," says Hank Zupnick, CIO of GE Real Estate. Yet, all too often, companies do not make the outlays required to make offshore outsourcing work.

"You have to bring people to America to learn your applications, and that takes time, particularly if you're doing it with a new vendor for the first time," explains Zupnick, who maintains a handful of three-year contracts with offshore vendors. In GE Real Estate's case, the transition time for each vendor was up to a year in some cases, in addition to the money-draining vendor selection period of several months.

Zupnick, who has seven years of offshore experience, says most of his peers don't appreciate the time and money it takes to get a relationship up and running. "The vendors say you can throw it over the wall and start saving money right away," he explains. "As a result, I've heard of CIOs who have tried to go the India or China route, and nine months later they pulled the plug because they weren't saving money. You have to build in up to a year for knowledge transfer and ironing out cultural differences."

At GE Real Estate, managing the offshore vendor is such a big task that Zupnick assigned someone to handle it on a half-time basis at a $50,000 salary. The individual makes sure projects move forward and develops and analyzes vendor proposals against the RFPs when it comes time to bid out new work.

Source: Adapted from Stephanie Overby, "The Hidden Costs of Offshore Outsourcing," *CIO* (September 1, 2003).

Cost Benefits of Internal and External Implementations

The costs of implementing a BPO project can be mitigated using a variety of tactics, depending in part on whether the implementation is handled internally or externally. Internal implementation will provide the value-adding benefits of increased levels of organizational learning and capability. The internal outsourcing manager or management team will be involved in drafting and distributing the RFP, responding to vendor inquiries, selecting a vendor, and initiating the BPO transition. Developing internal knowledge of these aspects of an implementation means the organization has acquired the capacity for additional BPO initiatives in the future. The greatest value-added benefit is likely to be the reduced time necessary for future BPO implementations, as well as a more effective implementation phase overall.

Cost mitigation benefits associated with hiring a consultant to conduct the BPO implementation include a faster process and, quite likely, a more effective vendor relationship. Professional service firms skilled in matching client needs with vendor capacities are likely to be able to provide significant value to the BPO buyer. The BPO buyer can derive even greater benefits if the consultant is compensated in part based on vendor performance. This is just one example of contracting mechanisms and innovations that can be used during the implementation phase to reduce risks and increase benefits.

Transition-Phase Costs

The transition phase is one in which the business process that formerly had been handled in house is wholly or in part shifted to the outsourcing vendor. The costs associated with this phase are driven by five primary characteristics of the BPO buyer—vendor relationship (Exhibit 3.4).

EXHIBIT 3.4

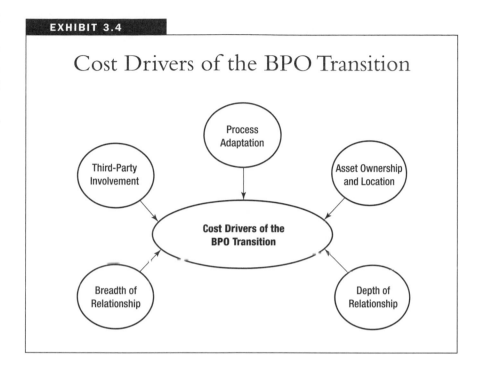

Cost Drivers of the BPO Transition

Process Adaptation

Third-Party Involvement

Asset Ownership and Location

Cost Drivers of the BPO Transition

Breadth of Relationship

Depth of Relationship

Asset Ownership and Location

The asset ownership and location driver concerns which firm will be better able to leverage people, technology, and other assets for competitive advantage, and where those assets should be located. In some situations, a BPO buyer may want to retain all or part of its existing assets to continue to develop internal competence in a process. For example, a firm may elect to outsource part of its call center function to a vendor as a means of freeing internal call center staff time to improve the in-house operation.

The decision about how asset ownership will be allocated between buyer and vendor has cost implications. For example, by outsourcing asset ownership, an organization can turn capital into expense: Assets that had previously required maintenance and continuing investment of time, money, equipment, and people are converted into a variable or fixed cost on the income statement, depending on the type of BPO contract.

The decision about where assets will be located also has cost implications. Retaining a process on the buying organization's premises usually means that the transition can be completed more quickly than by moving assets off-site, but not necessarily. There are many advantages to keeping assets on-site, including the fact that it is far easier to retain existing personnel, many of whom would be unwilling to relocate to the vendor (especially if the vendor is overseas). Employees involved in a process that has been outsourced can become productive members of the vendor organization, but the transition must be handled with care. It is not unusual for the BPO buyer to experience attrition, staff cuts, and reassignments during the transition phase. The vendor will often reengineer the outsourced process, reducing inefficiencies and enhancing individual productivity levels. This means that staff who remain may harbor lingering fears for their own job security—fears that may slow the transition and affect productivity. Proper management of the in-house transition to vendor management and process ownership will reduce these potential costs.

Regardless of whether the process remains on- or off-site, there will be a need to transfer process-related information, knowledge, and controls. During the transition phase it will also be necessary to establish information exchange and data interface protocols that mesh the existing standards and information management architectures of each firm. It is nearly inevitable that this integration process will have a variety of workflow disruptions. Data needed for routine tasks may be unavailable from time to time during the transition. New interface procedures, such as logins or passwords, may create confusion and frustration. The better the organization communicates with employees about these potential disruptions and their duration and scope, the less costly the transition phase will be.

Depth of Relationship

Depth of relationship refers to the costs associated with developing and maintaining a strategic relationship with the vendor. The nature of a strategic relationship between buyer and vendor is discussed in detail in the "Strategic Costs" section later in this chapter; however, it should be noted that a commitment to developing such a relationship will be more costly depending on the expectations for value extraction. The greater the value expected to be extracted from the relationship, the more time and resources will be required to develop and maintain the relationship.

Breadth of Relationship

The breadth of the relationship between buyer and vendor refers to the range of processes that are outsourced. In some cases, organizations outsource multiple functions to a single provider. In others, multiple providers are used for a range of different processes. The decision about the breadth of processes to outsource to a particular vendor has both direct and hidden costs. In fact, working with a single provider for multiple processes may reduce costs as familiarity and trust develop. At the same time, the potential costs associated with vendor failure increase as dependence on the vendor increases.

Third-Party Involvement

A potentially significant cost associated with the transition phase of the BPO initiative is based on the need for third parties to assist in the integration of both the vendor's and the initiating organization's systems. For example, it may be necessary to bring in specialists if the two firms have complex databases built on different platforms. This is more likely if the initiating organization has legacy systems that have not been upgraded in several years or if it has homegrown applications that are known only to a handful of individuals. The vendor should be expected to provide transition management expertise for most systems but cannot be expected to have the expertise to manage a smooth transition if the initiating organization has outdated or very old databases and information architectures. In that case, third parties may be necessary to assist in upgrading and migrating the buyer organization's data to the vendor's system.

Process Adaptation

Hidden costs associated with the transition phase center on the effects that outsourcing a process can have on employees who work outside that process. Employees may experience a period of adjustment as the process is transitioned. Adjustments include not only the need to understand and work with a reengineered process but also the need to interface with new people and unfamiliar systems. As usual for organizational change of this magnitude, some people will take longer than others to adjust, and some will simply resist the changes altogether. In general, organizations initiating a BPO project can expect some productivity dropoff in personnel who work internally with the outsourced process. Of course, the expectation is that after the period of adjustment, the productivity levels will reach their previous norms—and may even reach new highs as the efficiencies of the newly outsourced process kick in.

How the Process Reverses Negative Effects

Transition-phase costs are mitigated by the fact that the BPO decision has been made and the wheels of change set in motion. Although organization change creates possible productivity-sapping dangers, the negative effect is usually reversed once the organization is clearly pursuing its new objectives. Those who had resisted the change will either adjust or, at least, stop resisting. Resistance to organizational change—or, for that matter, to nearly any type of personal change—usually reaches a peak just before the decision to move forward. Once the decision is made, the mental energy that had previously been applied to blocking or resisting the change is now committed to adapting and adjusting to the new way of doing business—or to moving on to a new employer.[5]

Other cost mitigation strategies during the transition phase are, once again, associated with whether the process is handled internally. Internal management increases the organization's operational capabilities for additional BPO projects or other major change efforts. The transition phase is characterized by complexities of integrating management styles, information systems, and work cultures. Third-party consultants can assist in making the BPO transition easier and less time consuming. In the short run, hiring third-party support for the BPO transition can reduce costs. Organizations that are initiating BPO for the first time may want to hire a service provider, but should also assign a high-ranking insider to work closely with the consultant to siphon off knowledge that can be used to manage subsequent BPO projects internally.

Operational-Phase Costs

The operational phase of the BPO project refers to the period when the contract is being fully implemented and performance expectations drive the relationship. Among the endpoints that should be monitored as part of an ongoing BPO initiative are both financial and productivity ratios. Financial ratios that should be monitored range from standard return on investment (ROI) to margin enhancement. Depending on the intentions of the BPO project, the financial ratios to be monitored will vary slightly. As mentioned, some BPO projects are undertaken primarily for cost-reduction purposes and others primarily for strategic advantage purposes. Cost-reduction BPO projects are intended to enhance margins through reduced overhead, which can often be achieved within 6 to 12 months after commencement of the contract.

In contrast, strategic BPO attempts to leverage the world-leading capabilities of the outsourcing partner and focuses more on new revenue over margin enhancement. Organizations must establish financial metrics appropriate to the intentions of their BPO project. Exhibit 3.5 identifies key financial performance metrics associated with each type of BPO project.

Impact on Productivity

BPO implementation will have not only a financial impact on the organization but also a productivity impact. The productivity impact, it must be

EXHIBIT 3.5

Financial Performance Metrics

Cost-Reduction BPO	Strategic BPO
ROI	ROI
Net Margin	Gross Revenue
Sales/Employee	Market Share
Inventory Turns	Customer Acquisition Cost

noted, will likely reach beyond the unit or function that is targeted for outsourcing. Most BPO initiatives result in some job displacement or layoffs. Remaining employees will be concerned about whether their unit is a future BPO target. Those who are concerned about job security are likely to demonstrate a dropoff in productivity—at least in the short term.

Productivity measures used to control the BPO initiative must account for these short-term fluctuations in overall productivity while keeping track of long-term objectives. The distinction in metrics between cost-reduction BPO and strategic BPO is less pronounced for productivity than for financial indicators. Productivity measures are fairly consistent for the organization regardless of the cost-cutting or strategic initiatives undertaken. Organizations can use several important productivity metrics to control a BPO initiative, including:

- Output/employee
- Overhead cost/unit of output
- Output/capital expenditure
- Output/asset

These standard productivity measures will enable the firm to assess the pre- and post-BPO impact. The measures must each include a time element to account for short-term variation. It would be a mistake to pull the plug on a BPO initiative based on early returns that showed a dip in overall organizational productivity. Such fluctuation should be anticipated and accounted for before launching the project. Still, normalization or improvement in productivity should be expected within a pre-established period and adjustments made to the BPO initiative if those targets are not being met.

Internal Factors to Monitor

Qualitative measures of the BPO initiative are far-reaching, including internal, external, and vendor-related metrics. Internal qualitative metrics will focus on a variety of issues concerning the relative health of the organization. Effectively managing the BPO rollout will require data collection before, during, and after the process. Before the process begins, organizations should collect data on several characteristics of the internal environment. These include:

- Employee knowledge of BPO
- Employee understanding of organizational strategy
- Employee morale and sense of job security
- Employee capacity to deal with change

These various data points will help establish appropriate information and communication programs during and after BPO implementation. For example, if it is determined that employee knowledge of BPO and its potential to help the organization is low, the organization may benefit from training programs aimed at reducing the knowledge gap. Research has clearly shown that people are more productive and likely to pitch in throughout a change process if they understand the rationale and direction of the change.

Three Key External Audiences

External factors to monitor include issues related to customers, competitors, and shareholders. Organizations as a rule should be collecting data regarding customer satisfaction. However, it is critical that they maintain a close watch on customer satisfaction levels during BPO implementation, regardless of whether the BPO initiative involves a customer-facing function. Of course, normal variations in satisfaction levels should not precipitate corrective actions, but variations beyond the norm must be carefully analyzed in case action is required. The latter is especially important if the BPO initiative involves a customer-facing process such as a call center or help desk.

If the organization has undertaken a strategic BPO initiative, competitive response will be a crucial external variable to monitor. Strategic BPO is undertaken precisely to gain and, ideally, to sustain competitive advantage. Competitors will respond to new moves within the industry, especially those that have potential market-shifting or disruptive capability. Careful monitoring of the competition can help determine whether the rollout strategy is working.

Organizations should also monitor the reactions of shareholders and other major organizational stakeholders to the BPO initiative. Because most investors have a conservative streak, extensive reengineering or restructuring that includes a technology component may meet with anxiety and doubt. Clear understanding of stakeholder knowledge of organizational strategy before and after the BPO initiative has begun can help

TIPS & TECHNIQUES

BPO Rollout in a Competitive Climate

Given that a BPO initiative has the potential to alter the competitive climate, anyone undertaking the BPO implementation should be careful when developing a rollout plan. Organizations initiating BPO for strategic reasons will be wise to establish a rollout program that keeps them beneath competitors' radar screens—at least until a defensible position has been established.

circumvent unnecessary roadblocks that may arise as people hear about the outsourcing project.

Complex Buyer–Vendor Relationship

The final qualitative data points that must be collected involve those between the organization and the BPO partner. This complex relationship will evolve over time as the BPO partner performs on its contract. Underlying each BPO partner relationship are the so-called service-level agreements (SLAs) that specify actions to be taken to ensure customer satisfaction. Organizations often have only a few individuals who have read and understood the SLAs, and even fewer who know where they have been filed. If something goes wrong—and it always will—the SLAs will detail corrective actions. An organization should carefully monitor performance on the SLAs—both its own capacity for enforcing them and the vendor's capacity for responding to problems. A more detailed discussion of SLAs follows in Chapter 4.

Hidden costs associated with developing and maintaining the buyer–vendor relationship concern interpersonal skill issues. The needs and service requirements of an ongoing BPO will evolve over time, and the scope and nature of the buyer–vendor relationship must adapt as well. The typical BPO relationship lasts four to six years and involves continuing negotiations and deal making. Each of these encounters has the potential to incur undue costs resulting from poor negotiating skills, an incomplete or poorly designed original contract, or a rotating lead-person tango by either the BPO buyer or vendor.

Poor negotiating skills can lead to less-than-favorable terms on changes in the original contract or in the provision of new services. Poorly crafted original contracts can lock an organization into low service levels or draconian pricing. A rotating lead person by either party can mean a loss of organizational learning and a need to return repeatedly to the fundamentals underlying the relationship. This process is time consuming and can erode the cost advantages that are commonly part of a BPO relationship.

Strategic Costs

The strategic costs associated with BPO center on the potential loss of organizational learning that results from placing a process under the control of an external service provider. Outsourcing so-called noncore processes must be undertaken with careful forethought because it is never clear how future competitive conditions will unfold and what types of competencies will be required. As discussed in Chapter 2, firms must distinguish noncore activities as critical, key, or support. Those activities that are tightly coupled to the core and are fault intolerant (i.e., mission-critical processes) should usually be retained in-house. At the very least, they should be outsourced only when the interorganizational relationship is clearly focused on developing and deriving strategic advantages. Knowledge management should be transparent from one firm to the other, and reciprocal exchange of insights should be considered routine. Furthermore, a quest for innovation in the interlinking of the critical and core processes must be a paramount concern for both sides of the outsourcing relationship.

In fact, the major strategic component of a BPO initiative is the relationship between buyer and vendor. Relationship costs are those that are involved in courting, establishing, and maintaining a relationship with a BPO vendor.[6] This complex undertaking can be as far-reaching and comprehensive as a merger or joint venture. Such transactions are distinguished by the need to mesh information systems, governance structures, and organizational cultures into a unified whole. The complexity of the challenges of merging two formerly distinct enterprises is often too overwhelming for the executives who engineered the deal. One or more top executives are often either asked or forced to leave as they become increasingly disoriented amid the chaos of the combined entity. For example, the merger of Hewlett-Packard and Compaq in 2002 led to a quick departure of Compaq's then–CEO Michael Capellas.[7] Departures related to that merger continued well into 2003.[8]

A thoroughgoing BPO relationship can share many of the complexities of a major merger or joint venture. Firms that determine to outsource back-office processes are entering into a relationship with a vendor that will have important competitive implications. The risk posed by this loss of functional independence requires careful prior analysis of the capabilities and integrity of the vendor. In the case of a BPO relationship, it is simply unacceptable for any breakdowns in performance or integrity to occur.

Costs of a BPO Relationship

The directly attributable costs of a BPO relationship are those associated with identification, analysis, and selection of the various vendor candidates; controlling the vendor relationship; and developing strategic knowledge management capacities with the vendor.

Hidden costs associated with the vendor relationship are primarily centered on the impact of transitioning formerly internal processes to external control. For example, in many outsourcing relationships, employees of the BPO buyer become employees of the vendor. This is often the case in data center management wherein a large organization such as EDS simply acquires the existing IT infrastructure, including staff, from the outsourcer.[9] This transition from one employer to another can have ripple effects throughout the organization, as uncertainty and fear are typically associated with changes of this type.[10] Others near to or friendly with those who have a new employer may pick up on grumbling or criticism and wonder if they will be next in line for such a transition. In other words, the social contract between employer and employee—whether explicit or tacit—has the appearance of being violated when employees are optioned to another firm. It does not matter that such optioning usually results in better efficiencies and working conditions. The perceived violation of the social contract is enough to send some employees scurrying to Monster.com to seek out a new employer. The disruption of the work environment will always have hidden costs as morale and productivity are negatively affected by change.

Avoiding a Cat-and-Mouse Game on Strategic Costs

Strategic costs associated with outsourcing can be mitigated through appropriate vendor selection and contracting. Using stringent selection procedures ensures that the vendor chosen has the intellectual, technological, and social resources to become a true partner in the success of the BPO buyer. The buyer–vendor relationship should not become a cat-and-mouse game focused on price issues. Rather, both sides should work to create positive-sum outcomes from their deep relationship. That is, rather than constantly seeking to increase service prices, the vendor should seek ways to help the buyer grow and to participate in that growth. Likewise, rather than constantly beating down the vendor's price, the BPO buyer should seek to deepen the partnership and find ways to leverage the vendor's capacity for mutual benefit. This is not a typical buyer–supplier relationship as outlined in the standard strategy textbooks.

Applying the TCM Model

The costs associated with a BPO initiative are many, and they can easily overwhelm a project and the project manager if they are not anticipated in advance. The TCM model discussed earlier places costs within the context of project phases. Thus, at different points during the BPO initiative, it can be determined whether costs are in line with expectations and/or whether adjustments need to be made.

Exhibit 3.6 illustrates how costs can be mapped to BPO project phases. In many cases, the costs incurred directly in one phase linger across the other phases. Hidden costs and opportunity costs are present

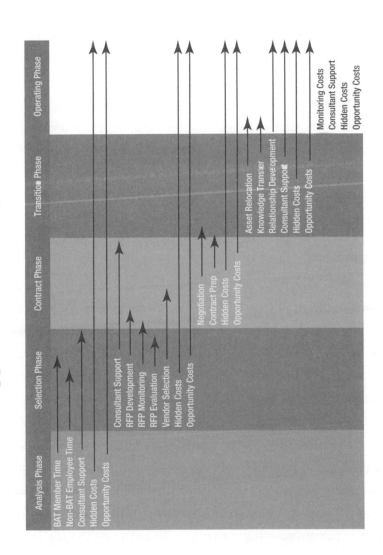

EXHIBIT 3.6

TCM Applied to BPO Project Phases

in each phase, and they have lasting effects that accumulate over time and must be estimated to get a true idea of BPO costs.

BPO project costs should be tracked throughout and adjustments in projected and actual total costs modified along the way. If savings have been achieved over anticipated costs, they should be noted just as cost overruns should be noted. Cost savings may be a good thing, but they may also be a warning indicator that an important consideration in the BPO project has been overlooked. Smart managers are cost alert and employ mitigation tactics wherever possible. They are also aware that every major change initiative carries risks and costs before benefits can be realized. This essential tension between moving forward and pulling the plug should motivate constant cost vigilance and a culture of appropriate frugality.

Summary

The costs of a BPO project go far beyond mere labor-cost arbitrage. They occur at all four levels of the process—analysis, implementation, transition, and maintenance—and can be categorized as either financial or strategic costs. One technique for identifying, forecasting, and mitigating these costs is total cost management (TCM), an effective tool for recognizing overt as well as hidden costs. There are a number of critical factors in the cost equation, including decisions about whether to handle BPO internally or externally, development of RFPs and review of responses, and how well initiating organizations create and sustain positive relationships with vendors. At the same time, an organization must consider impacts on internal (employee) as well as external stakeholders to help maximize competitive benefits of the BPO project.

Endnotes

1. Nick J. Lavingia, "Improve Profitability Through Effective Project Management and Total Cost Management," *Cost Engineering* 45, no. 11 (November 2003): 22–24.

2. Alex Arthur, "How to Build Your Project Budget," *Management Accounting* (April 2000): 20–22.

3. Charles C. Denova, "The Hawthorne Effect," *Training & Development* (October 1968): 46–49.

4. Many researchers question the validity of the so-called Hawthorne studies and the reliability of the so-called Hawthorne effect. See for example, John G. Adair, "The Hawthorne Effect: A Reconsideration of the Methodological Artifact," *Journal of Applied Psychology* (May 1984): 334–345.

5. Robert Kegan and Lisa Laskow Lahey, "The Real Reason People Won't Change," *Harvard Business Review* (November 2001): 84–91.

6. Arnold B. Maltz and Lisa M. Ellram, "Total Cost of Relationship: An Analytical Framework for the Logistics Outsourcing Decision," *Journal of Business Logistics* 18, no. 1 (1997): 45–65.

7. Keith Regan, "Capellas to Leave HP—for Worldcom?" *E-Commerce Times* (November 12, 2002).

8. Tom Krazit, HP Integration Team Leader Resigns," *IDG News Service* (November 25, 2003).

9. Mark Jones and Brian Fonseca, "EDS: Outsourcing Still a Money Spinner," *NetworkWorldFusion* (January 18, 2002).

10. Michael Useem and Joseph Harder, "Leading Laterally in Company Outsourcing," *Sloan Management Review* (Winter 2000): 25–36.

CHAPTER 4

Vendor Selection
and Contracting

 After reading this chapter, you will be able to:

- Undertake a systematic approach to identifying and selecting the right vendor for a BPO project
- Establish a vendor selection team and develop its charter
- Develop a list of potential vendors, acquire the necessary information from them, then cull the list to the most likely prospects
- Recognize the criteria for selection—and know when not to make a selection
- Manage the critical stage between vendor selection and development of the contract
- Recognize the difference between negotiating an outsourcing contract and a traditional commercial contract
- Focus on the 11 key components of an outsourcing contract, and know how to consider and include them for maximum organizational advantage

Finding the right BPO vendor and developing an appropriate contract are essential to an organization's outsourcing initiative. Regarding the former, the promise of BPO is always tempered by the perceived risks associated with handing responsibility for an internal business process— no matter how noncore or mundane it may be—to another firm. So getting the right partner is crucial. As to the latter, careful consideration of the elements in an effective outsourcing contract can help avoid many of the risks that contribute to BPO failure. The fact is, managing these functions in a way that reflects the strategic nature of the buyer–vendor relationship—that is, with an eye toward mutual satisfaction, trust, and precision—can go a long way toward maximizing the potential for BPO success.

Identifying and Selecting the Right Vendor

The vendor identification and selection process has a life cycle of its own. It starts with scouring the Internet and other sources to identify potential vendors/partners, and continues through the stages of getting acquainted, evaluation, and selection. Although in some ways, this process is subjective—based in part on how well the buyer and vendor firms relate to one another—it can also be conducted systematically. Large firms, such as Xerox, that pioneered BPO have well-developed systematic approaches for identifying and selecting outsourcing vendors.[1] Fortunately, the systematic approach that has been pioneered by the large early adopters of BPO has been refined and standardized over time. The basic steps are now well known. This quasi-standardization means vendors have developed expectations of how they will be approached and how they will be required to bid on projects. Becoming familiar with the standard procedures of vendor selection, then, can speed the vendor review and selection process for buyers and vendors alike.

Eight Steps to Success

The vendor identification and selection process can be broken into eight steps:

1. Appoint a vendor selection team (VST).
2. Establish qualifications.
3. Develop a long list.
4. Distribute the request for information (RFI).
5. Distribute the request for proposals (RFP).
6. Evaluate proposals.
7. Select a short list.
8. Select a vendor.

There are a number of rationales for this process. The most obvious is that the BPO vendor relationship can be strategically important to the BPO buyer in the long term. Getting the right vendor from the start can accelerate the realization of strategic benefits associated with an effective BPO relationship. A systematic process is also more likely to reveal the various alternatives in the market and help the buyer distinguish among service options. As more and more outsourcing providers enter the market, they are developing increasingly sophisticated means of differentiating themselves, often around the services they provide.[2] The dynamics of the BPO vendor market, and the ease of entry for new firms with innovative new approaches, makes a systematic selection process nearly imperative.

Step 1: Appoint a Vendor Selection Team

There is far more to choosing an outsourcing vendor than there is to choosing a new supplier. Unlike the buyer–supplier relationship, the BPO buyer–vendor relationship involves a customized service, detailed agreement on service levels, and a strategically oriented long-term contract. The buyer and vendor must have shared interests in key objectives and values. The relationship will be more intimate. In general, BPO buyer–vendor relationships are characterized by regular senior management meetings and sharing of otherwise confidential information. Therefore, harmony among each firm's predominant management styles is vital.

After the BPO Analysis Team (BAT) identifies the BPO opportunity, estimated costs, and built the business case for an outsourcing project, a new team—or at least new team charter—should be developed for the vendor selection process. This is the vendor selection team (VST), which will work in relationship with other BPO project teams (Exhibit 4.1).

Organizations may elect to keep the BAT intact for the vendor selection process or elect to develop a new team. Many firms decide to empower and charter a new team to manage partnership identification, selection, and development to introduce fresh ideas and provide a clear endpoint to the BAT's efforts. But regardless of whether a new team is

EXHIBIT 4.1

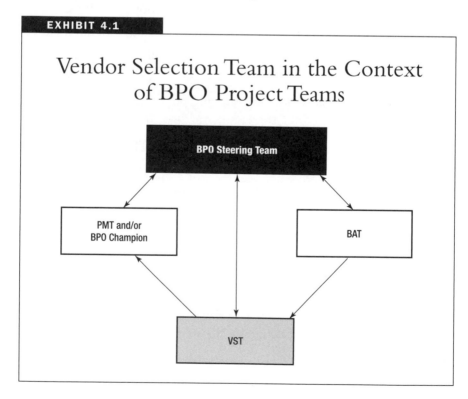

Vendor Selection Team in the Context of BPO Project Teams

established, the organization should consciously select and develop one or more individuals to serve as BPO champions, at least one of which should come from the BAT. These champions will be in charge of developing and deepening the outsourcing relationship over the long term. Experience has shown that it is better to have the BPO champion

TIPS & TECHNIQUES

Establishing a VST Charter

As with any formally chartered team within the organization, the VST should establish a regular meeting schedule and set clear goals and objectives. Here is a sample VST charter:

- Purpose: To undertake a process of identifying and selecting a vendor to provide outsourcing services in the area identified by the BPO Analysis Team.
- Goals:
  - To develop a list of qualifications that the BPO vendor will minimally require
  - To identify a long list of potential vendors
  - To gather information and evaluate the list of vendors
  - To develop an RFP and evaluate proposals from the list of vendors
  - To select a short list of vendors
  - To select a final vendor candidate and evaluate its ability to meet the performance goals indicated in the RFP
- Objectives:
  - To complete the long list in 30 days
  - To gather information and evaluate long-list vendors in 30 days
  - To develop the RFP in 15 days
  - To solicit and review vendor proposals in 60 days
  - To review short-list candidates in 30 days
  - To select a vendor within six months

emerge from the vendor identification and selection team than to bring one in later to manage the ongoing relationship.[3]

Draw VST Members from Key Staff

The VST should draw from the business areas that will be affected by the BPO project. Key staff members for the VST should include:

- Senior management
- Legal staff with contract expertise
- Technical staff and information systems analysts
- End users
- Financial staff

Consulting firms are available to help the VST with defining statements of work, evaluating internal needs, negotiating, evaluating vendor performance, and providing quality assurance. Although these services represent additional costs, they can enable the organization to reduce risks, accomplish goals, and select the right BPO partner.

Step 2: Establish Qualifications

It is imperative for the BPO buyer to establish minimum vendor qualifications. These may include standard items such as experience, price, and location, as well as strategic items such as the vendor's organizational culture, decision-making style, and reputation. According to extensive research into what outsourcing buyers need, the qualifications most often sought in a vendor are:[4]

- Quality
- Performance history
- Warranties and claims policies
- Facilities and capacity
- Geographic location
- Technical capability

Who does ERISA adviser work? for employer of for flar ?

In addition to these, other factors come into play as well:

- *Customer service.* BPO buyers must maintain a *customer* mindset to derive as much value as possible from the vendor and avoid making concessions on provisions it has established as necessary for the project. A *partner* mindset in the BPO buyer should emerge only after the vendor has been selected and the contracting process has begun. In the partnership development stage of a BPO relationship, mutual compromise and cooperation is expected.

- *Process expertise.* This becomes less important the further from the core the outsourced process is. Processes that are close to the outsourcing organization's core competence should never be outsourced to an inexperienced vendor.

- *Data sharing.* Given that data sharing between the various commercial databases can be difficult, the technology platform of the vendor should be a qualification. If vendors do not have a system that is easily compatible with the buyer's existing system, they should be responsible for demonstrating how that hurdle can be overcome.

- *Vendor's business.* Understanding the emphasis of a vendor's business, or what drives its revenue, is critical. For example, large vendors usually look for large contracts. Smaller contracts negotiated with large vendors are unlikely to receive the same quality of treatment as larger contracts.

- *Industry specialization.* Any vendor, other than the major consultancies, that claims to specialize in several outsourcing service areas should be treated with caution. Having a large base of multifunctional outsourcing expertise is rare, not to mention expensive to maintain. Many vendors will say that the skills from outsourcing a function in one industry transfer to another, and that may well be the case. But, in general, if the vendor is not an expert in the field, it will not know about the hidden challenges associated with providing services in that industry.

- *Specificity.* Firms interested in specific types of BPO providers can stipulate that as a qualification. Some buyers may not want to use an offshore provider, for example. Others may specifically prefer the so-called pure play vendor, who specializes in a single business process. Still others may desire a shared-services provider, who serves multiple clients from a centralized location and usually bases its fees on a "pay by the pound" basis.

Whatever qualifications the VST establishes, those critical to the buyer should be decided at this early stage in the selection process. At minimum, the requisite qualifications should consider both expected performance levels and strategic fit with the buyer organization. Many firms also distinguish qualifications between *soft* and *hard* issues. *Soft issues* include cultural and organizational values, mission and vision statements, and organizational history. *Hard issues* are more quantitative and are usually associated with performance and productivity. In addition to this distinction, some firms also use a weight system to distribute the relative importance of each issue over the decision process (Exhibit 4.2).

Step 3: Develop a Long List

The VST's objective is to build a list of 15 to 20 qualified potential vendors. By searching for and evaluating multiple vendors, BPO buyers will better understand what the marketplace has to offer, will be more likely to find vendors best suited for their project, and will distribute risk over multiple partners.

There are several good places to start the BPO vendor search, including—believe it or not—the Internet. The VST can make headway in vendor identification by using the standard Internet search engines and keyword combinations. Another approach is to search among current suppliers to see if any are qualified and willing to bid on the BPO project. This type of relationship is referred to as *sole sourcing* or *single sourcing* and can be effective based on a shared experience of working together. However, sole sourcing may lead to retaining a vendor that is not completely qualified to manage the business process under consideration. It

EXHIBIT 4.2

Sample VST Charter

Purpose

To undertake a process of identifying and selecting a vendor to provide outsourcing services in the area identified by the BPO Analysis Team.

Goals

1. To develop a list of qualifications that the BPO vendor will minimally require.
2. To identify a long list of potential vendors.
3. To gather information and evaluate the long list of vendors.
4. To develop an RFP and evaluate proposals from the long list of vendors.
5. To select a short list of vendors.
6. To select a final vendor candidate and evaluate its ability to meet the performance goals indicated in the RFP.

Objectives

1. To complete the long list in 30 days.
2. To gather information and evaluate long-list vendors in 30 days.
3. To develop the RFP in 15 days.
4. To solicit and review vendor proposals in 60 days.
5. To review short-list candidates in 30 days.
6. To select a vendor within 6 months.

TIPS & TECHNIQUES

Importance of Being Clandestine

The long-list development process is generally conducted in a semi-clandestine (at least to the outside world) manner. If the BPO buyer reveals it is in the market for a BPO vendor, it is not unusual to be overwhelmed with unsolicited proposals. In many cases a new BPO vendor search can generate three or more times the proposals desired.

also increases risk. If the vendor faces problems, more of the BPO buyer's processes will be affected.

Many outsourcing magazines and online portals offer unbiased directories to assist in locating potential vendors. These include Outsourcing-Central.com, Outsourcing Center, the Outsourcing Institute, and FirmBuilder. BPO buyers may want to consider third-party consultants, some of whom offer free searches and have built a list of vendors from which to choose. Additionally, buyers can also find vital information—case studies, lists of partners, customers, services, and so on—on the respective Web sites of potential long-list vendor candidates.

Step 4: Request for Information

After gathering the necessary data to identify 15 to 20 potential BPO vendors, it is time to begin culling the list. This involves directly gathering information from the candidates. A common technique to accomplish this is to send a scope of work (SOW) outline specification and request for information (RFI) to each vendor on the long list. The SOW should contain the broad intention of the outsourcing proposal and the time frame for responding. The RFI is a questionnaire-type survey intended to establish the level of vendor competence and interest.

One method for contacting long-list vendors is via a phone call to the sales department. This will involve only a high-level discussion about the BPO project and is designed to assess the vendor's interest before moving forward with the RFI. If there is interest, specific information should be gathered about where and to whom the RFI should be sent. The vendor should also be informed as to whether the buyer would allow a dialog before the RFI process.

Capabilities Interview

The VST should set a firm deadline for responding to the RFI. After it has passed, the VST will schedule and conduct capabilities interviews with acceptable respondents to determine their ability to meet project goals. Capabilities interviews are conducted initially via conference call. Questions that need to be addressed during this call include:

- What are the vendor's core capabilities?
- What metrics does the vendor use to evaluate its effectiveness?
- How many clients is the vendor currently serving?
- Does the vendor have unused capacity or will it have to grow to serve new clients?
- Where is the vendor investing its resources?
- How well does the vendor rate with its current customers?
- Does the vendor fit with the buying company's culture?

During this assessment, the BPO buyer should determine which vendors have the skills, technology, and personnel necessary to fulfill the project. A vendor site visit will assist with this determination. If a site visit is warranted, the VST should meet with vendor management teams and personnel, evaluate their workplace, and observe how they respond to requests and questions. The long list should be reduced by half after the interviews, leaving 7 to 10 vendors. The VST should inform them of their selection to receive the formal RFP.

Step 5: Request for Proposals

The objective of developing an RFP is to create a document that details the services, activities, and performance targets required for the BPO project. But the RFP is also a sales document designed to interest vendors who can add value to the BPO buyer organization. Although RFPs vary in format, at minimum they should clearly communicate project requirements to ensure that initial responses provide a full and unambiguous picture of the vendor's abilities, sophistication, and experience.

General RFP Guidelines

There are several general guidelines for developing an effective RFP. One of the most important is to be clear about the business process slated for outsourcing and the scope of work required from the vendor. At the same time, RFPs should not be so long and burdensome that some qualified vendors will elect not to respond. Several items that should be included are:

- *Administrative.* This section includes information about the BPO buyer's company, business priorities, purpose of the RFP, deadlines for response, required format, assessment criteria, and contact information.

- *General requirements.* This section details expectations regarding the services to be provided, reporting and information sharing, customer service, claims resolution, contract implementation, training, and benchmarks for fees. For example, a firm that is seeking to outsource its help desk function might have a section including details about the function (Exhibit 4.3).

- *Pricing requirements.* This section outlines the expected pricing approach, including goals for net rates and volume discounts.

- *Contractual/legal.* This section provides details about expected contract terms and conditions, warranties, remedies, and any disclaimers.

Generally speaking, the VST should be able to eliminate two or three from the list after reviewing the bids, because some vendors' skills will not match the project needs. A letter should be sent out immediately to the eliminated vendors. This will leave five to eight remaining for further evaluation.

Step 6: Evaluate the Proposals

Initial screening of the proposals may reveal interesting facts about the vendor. For example, the VST should scan each one to determine if it addresses the organization's unique needs. Often, a BPO vendor will use

EXHIBIT 4.3

BPO Qualifications Weighting System

Parameter	Weight
Quality:	
• ISO Certification	.20
• Six Sigma	
Performance History:	
• Experience with other, similar projects	.25
• Performance with other clients	
Warranties and Claims Policies	.10
Facilities and Capacity	.15
Geographic Location	.05
Technical Capability	.25

a generic template or cut and paste material from another proposal and simply insert it in the current one. This often indicates the vendor has not focused specifically on what the buyer needs. A good BPO vendor must be customer oriented, and the proposal should be directly written for the buyer's project.

Second Telephone Interview

Remaining vendors should be scheduled for telephone interviews of about one hour in length. During this teleconference, the vendor should explain its proposal in detail, including addressing issues such as:

- Approach
- Company background
- Experience in the process area
- Strengths
- Availability

- Certifications
- Suggested solution

The VST should then request a submission of tender and set a firm deadline for its receipt. The tender is a precise document that spells out exactly what the vendor intends to do and how it intends to establish fees and the invoice schedule. The vendor should also be requested to furnish:

- *Case studies.* These should reflect projects similar to the BPO buyer's project.

- *Copies of resumes.* Each vendor will probably send resumes of its best personnel. The buyer should ensure that these individuals will actually work on the project.

- *Copies of certifications.* BPO vendors often cite industry certifications, such as ISO or Six Sigma. Buyers should request copies of these certificates to verify their authenticity.

- *References.* Buyers should request at least three positive references and, when possible, one negative reference. It is important that the BPO buyer talk with at least one of the vendor's customers that experienced a negative result. This will help determine how the vendor handled the project when it was failing and why contingency plans did not correct the problems.

- *Proof of financial stability.* It is not unusual to request that vendors provide documentation showing their financial stability, number of employees, how long they have been in business, and the maturity of their facilities.

Step 7: Select a Short List

The VST should now have enough information to select the three to five most qualified vendors, who should be contacted and invited in for face-to-face formal presentations.

Vendor Presentation

The VST should meet with one vendor per day. The vendor visits should be limited to four hours and be scheduled as close together as possible so the VST can compare notes on each vendor while impressions are still fresh. The VST should set the meeting agenda and share it with each vendor in advance. At the beginning of the formal presentation, the VST chairperson should:

- Inform the vendor that it has made the short list.
- Explain that the vendor has four hours for its presentation.
- Express interest regarding the vendor's pricing model.
- Reiterate what the organization is looking for in a BPO vendor.
- Let the vendor know there will be a final telephone conference to clarify the bid submitted.
- Ask the vendor to submit its best bid no later than the deadline you have established.
- Let the vendor know when the decision will be made.

During the presentation, VST members should look for the following:

- Who has the vendor sent to the meeting?
- Is the presentation developed uniquely or canned?
- Does the vendor include contingency plans?
- What performance data does the vendor provide?
- Who are the vendor's leading clients?
- How well does the vendor team *listen* to the buyer team?
- Does the vendor's presentation address issues in the RFP?

Special attention should also be paid to the logical architecture outlined in the presentation. Many vendors demonstrate their technology expertise, but lack deep understanding of workflows and process improvement opportunities (the logical architecture). Failure to address the logical architecture of the business process being outsourced is one of the most obvious signs that a vendor lacks maturity in that process.

Final Review

After the presentations are over, the final review begins. The VST should review all presentation material in great detail, along with the notes recorded by those who attended the presentations. Someone within the VST should record all questions the team may have, as these can be answered in the final phone conferences with each vendor. This conference call is to clarify outstanding issues about the proposal and to discuss the formal presentation. During the call, the BPO buyer should communicate the following:

- Explain to the vendor that it is among the finalists.
- Explain that this will be the final presentation.
- State that final pricing schedules must be articulated.

The vendor should be allowed to ask questions. The buyer should state that a decision will be made and a vendor selected within a defined period (usually two weeks). This helps motivate the vendor into making the best deal possible to win the buyer's business.

After the conference, the buyer should select two or three vendors for a second face-to-face presentation. Once this selection has been made and the vendors have been informed, the meetings should be scheduled as soon as possible. Each vendor should be informed it has four hours for the final presentation.

Step 8: Select the Vendor

Final vendor selection should be completed shortly after the second round of face-to-face presentations. By this time, it is usually clear which vendor's proposal best meets the long- and short-term needs of the buyer. However, the VST may decide that none of the vendors is suitable. If that occurs, it is in the interest of the organization to abandon the

BPO project. For many executives and managers, this may be difficult given the investment of personal time and other resources. But sound business decision making sometimes requires firms to cut their losses and move on rather than gerrymandering the specifications or allowing the vendor to alter its bid to try to force a fit.

Precontract Stage

If a vendor is selected, there are still several steps to consider before moving to the contract stage:

- Members of the BPO buyer's staff who are scheduled for transfer to the vendor should meet the new management team before contracts are signed.

TIPS & TECHNIQUES

Make Time for Adjustments

A useful exercise is to ensure the contract will stand up to the rigors and complexities of the actual operation. A trial period is ideal for making adjustments before the contract becomes final and for judging the likelihood of the partnership's breaking down. In general, this period should not be less than 90 days—long enough to allow anything unexpected to arise.

For example, when Lehman Brothers decided to outsource its IT function to an offshore firm, it spent more than $8 million on 80 separate pilot projects with the various finalists.[a] Remember, the BPO buyer and vendor are attempting to develop a partnership, and there are going to be problems that must be worked through.

After the test period, the main issue that needs to be addressed is the unexpected work that has surfaced and how it will affect the vendor's cost proposal. At the same time, the buyer should be cautious about judging the service levels, because new people and processes will improve performance levels over time.

[a]Mario Apicella, "Shaking Hands Is Not Enough," InfoWorld (April 30, 2001): 49–50.

- Employees should be allowed to air concerns and ask questions. This can help reduce any feelings that they are being cast aside.

- The firms should address issues of terms and conditions of employment, including appropriate compensation if vendor employment is not available or not required.

- If additional training will be necessary as a result of joining the new organization, it should be brought to light.

- Leaders of the BPO implementation from both parties should discuss the objectives of the new work processes, reinforce what the organizations want to achieve, and understand how members of the interorganizational work teams will contribute to the team's success.

BPO Contract

First-time outsourcing projects fail to meet their objectives for reasons that are as varied and complex as outsourcing relationships themselves. And while failures are generally not strictly legal in nature, a poorly drafted contract is one of the most significant reasons cited for unsuccessful relationships. The careful negotiation and drafting of a good outsourcing contract can not only preserve the potential of an outsourcing project, but also minimize the risk of failure and eliminate most other points of dissatisfaction.

IN THE REAL WORLD

Rules of Thumb for Effective BPO Contracting

David S. Piper, attorney, Boyer & Ketchand, LLP, Houston, Texas, offers these guidelines for BPO contracting:

"First, everyone involved in the process should keep in mind the nature of the BPO relationship. The alignment of the long-term strategic interests of both the BPO buyer and vendor should be reflected in the terms of the contract.

"Second, it is important to be able to describe services and performance levels in precise language. The contract should include details about measuring service performance and steps to take to remedy performance shortfalls.

"Finally, it is important for the parties to plan for exit. This element of BPO contracts is often overlooked because it suggests that, at some point in the future, the relationship will end. However, handling exit provisions is a good way to make sure that when the relationship does end, it ends amicably.

"When it comes to common mistakes that companies make in developing an outsourcing contract, one is the failure to test performance metrics and measurement strategies. One firm that I recall outsourced its help desk process. Part of the agreement was that the quality of service would be measured using a help desk customer survey. The help desk vendor applied the quality survey to every single help desk inquiry, which greatly annoyed the BPO buyer's employees.

"To make matters worse, completion of the survey was required to close out the trouble ticket. As a result, help desk staff frequently called employees to implore them to answer the survey questions so they could close out the ticket. Overlooking the impact of the survey on the attitudes of employees led to a lot of criticism and needless griping in this case.

"A way to help keep legal costs to a minimum in BPO contract development—and this may sound paradoxical—is to get the legal team involved early. Early involvement ensures that the team is well versed in the business process and understands appropriate service levels metrics. Firms should also get the legal team involved with the operational staff so they don't end up writing the contract in the abstract. The more familiar the team is with the actual business process, the better it will be able to draft effective service level standards."

Source: David Piper, Boyer & Ketchand, Attorneys at Law, Houston, Texas.

Negotiating BPO Contracts

Although this discussion is intentionally brief and not designed to supplant the many excellent books written on the art of negotiation, it is important to examine the nature of negotiating BPO contracts.

The complexity and evolving nature of the outsourcing process demands a different mindset than is required in traditional commercial contract negotiation (Exhibit 4.4).[5] It is not a zero-sum game, in which each party is motivated to extract as much value as possible from the limited available resources, even to the detriment of the other party.[6] In these types of negotiations, the outcome is win–lose in that one party or the other gets its way. Although there may be clear advantages for the winner, the relationship is likely to become adversarial rather than collaborative. This probably will not promote the kind of long-term collaboration critical to successful BPO initiatives.

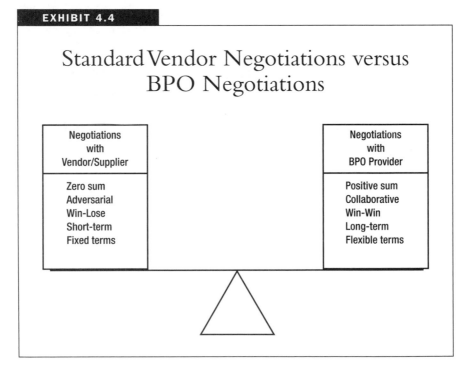

EXHIBIT 4.4

Standard Vendor Negotiations versus BPO Negotiations

Negotiations with Vendor/Supplier	Negotiations with BPO Provider
Zero sum Adversarial Win-Lose Short-term Fixed terms	Positive sum Collaborative Win-Win Long-term Flexible terms

However, developing an effective BPO contract requires a positive-sum approach whereby the parties are interested in creating more value than currently exists. It aims for the proverbial "win–win" outcome and seeks long-term, flexible contract terms. This requires compromise by both parties. At the same time, risks associated with compromise can be mitigated through creative incentive clauses and remedies in the event of nonperformance. Such contract innovations are part of the terms of a BPO contract.

A First Look

From the BPO buyer's perspective, selecting an outsourcing provider and negotiating the contract is also the first opportunity to evaluate the vendor's culture and mindset, and to determine if the fit is a good one. Buyers can use several strategies to determine the character of the firm they have selected. For example, different negotiating strategies may be employed to distinguish a cooperative vendor from an adversarial one. At the outset of the selection process, buyers may attach a proposed form of the master outsourcing contract (without detailed exhibits such as scope of work, service-level agreements, and pricing) to the RFP in order to evaluate which vendors will accept the general terms and conditions. Vendors unwilling or reluctant to accept these terms and conditions without significant negotiation can be readily identified and disqualified.

Terms of the Contract

Although BPO contract negotiations should be conducted in a positive-sum spirit, it would be naive to assume that trust is a sufficient governing mechanism. In fact, drafting precise contract terms, including avenues for remedy in case performance falls short of expectations, can help preserve a relationship during difficult stretches. The discussion that follows outlines terms that should be considered and included in the formal BPO contract. Although not an exhaustive set, the terms discussed are part of nearly every BPO contract and constitute the core of the working relationship. They include:

- Scope of work (SOW)
- Service-level agreements (SLAs)
- Pricing
- Term of the contract
- Governance
- Intellectual property
- Industry-specific concerns
- Termination of the contract
- Transition
- Force majeure
- Dispute resolution

Scope of Work

The linchpin of the contract is a description of the nature of the work being outsourced, often referred to as the *scope of work* or *statement of work*. The BPO buyer's attorneys must work closely with the buying organization's personnel to become intimately familiar with the details of the outsourced processes in order to prepare a clear, complete statement of work.

Provisions of a well-drafted contract should outline the change process as it pertains to the SOW, whether such change is incremental because of technological developments or organic because of acquisitions or divestitures by the client. They should also delineate the processes by which the work will be transitioned from buyer to vendor. Personnel, hard assets, and soft assets (intellectual property, vendor contracts, license agreements, etc.) all may be transferred to the vendor. Particular care must be taken in the personnel area as well. Employees with key institutional knowledge or other unique capabilities should be considered for retention. Well-qualified project managers must be retained to staff the buyer's governance team.

Awareness of Employment Laws Is Critical

Attention must also be paid to the employment laws that regulate the BPO vendor, especially when there is an international component to the project. In the European Union (EU), for example, in certain cases when a business unit is transferred, the new employer must offer transferred employees the same wages and benefits the employees have with their current employer. Staffing needs should be carefully considered, because layoffs and reductions in force are often more complicated in foreign jurisdictions. The EU has also enacted stiff laws that protect workers from loss of income if their employer should decide to outsource their jobs. The Applied Rights Directive is designed to protect employees' jobs, pay, and conditions when organizations sell or outsource parts of their business operations to other companies or contracting firms.

The United Kingdom has enacted similar legislation known as Transfer of Undertakings Protection of Employment (TUPE). These regulations are potent protectors of employment rights and can make it difficult for European firms to realize dramatic cost benefits from outsourcing.

Service-Level Agreements

In an SLA, a vendor agrees to achieve defined levels of performance (Exhibit 4.5). If the vendor fails to meet these objectives, the SLA provides the buyer with various rights and remedies. A carefully crafted set of SLAs aligns the interests of the vendor and buyer.[7] Poorly drafted SLAs almost ensure a failed relationship.[8]

Unfortunately, SLAs are among the most difficult of outsourcing contract provisions. A solid SLA requires an intimate understanding of business processes by the attorneys drafting the agreement (SLAs should not be drafted by nonlawyers). The parties must document in great detail the requirements of each outsourced process and agree on how to measure service levels and consequences for the failure to meet them.[9]

EXHIBIT 4.5

Sample Text for Service Level Agreements

Scope and Definition

Outsource contractor shall "own" continuation engineering for mature products, as agreed upon by the company and the outsource contractor. This will enable outsource contractor to design the product for a high volume assembly environment and with component parts sourced to take advantage of outsource contractor purchasing leverage. This is expected to drive significant cost reductions in future products.

Outsourcing Contractor Responsibilities

- Release bill of material for new SKU number.
- Assume responsibility for initiating, executing and implementing engineering change orders in support of ongoing product enhancements.
- Perform cross-functional cost reduction and product improvement activities.
- Provide technical assistance to Company in effecting resolutions to product quality problems.
- Provide a cost reduction plan to Company. The plan should include feasibility report, design study, and analysis of specifications.
- Support product "end of life" activities to minimize scrap and obsolescence.
- Review and approve component-level first article inspection.

Company Responsibilities

- Develop, maintain, and provide customer requirement specification.
- Approve key technology and engineering changes initiated by outsource contractor.
- Provide all specifications, artwork, and packaging of the products.
- Provide firmware support for outsource contractor-initiated and Company-approved engineering changes.

Defining What to Measure   The foundation of the SLA is defining which service levels and key performance indicators (KPIs) to measure. An SLA may be tied to anything that can be objectively quantified but is usually a measure of such indicators as quality, speed, availability, reliability, capacity, timeliness, or customer satisfaction. With a call center, for example, service levels might include the average time to answer a call, the duration of the call, the percentage of issues satisfactorily resolved in the first call, and customer satisfaction.

Service levels must be intimately tied to pricing in order to properly align the financial interests of the vendor and the business goals of the buyer. For example, pricing tied to the number of problems fixed may create a disincentive to stop the problems from happening in the first place. Quality is generally a better service-level measure than quantity, especially in fixed-price scenarios.

Precise Terms, Variables, and Responsibility   Once appropriate service levels are agreed on, terms must be used with precision. For example, what does it mean for a computer system to be "available"? If the buyer can access the system, but it performs sluggishly, is that system available? What if the system is unavailable to the buyer because of something beyond the vendor's control? Who bears the risk of a failed service level in that instance? Drilling down to issues such as these in the negotiation process will avoid needless disputes during the performance stage of the BPO initiative.

Service levels may vary depending on hours of operation or other variables. Response times should account for these factors, including differences in time zones. Agreement must be reached between the parties regarding how to measure service levels. Technologic capabilities may be a constraining factor, particularly with smaller buyers and vendors. Softer measurements, such as customer satisfaction, may meet with resistance, both from the vendor and from the buyer's personnel who are now required to fill out satisfaction surveys as a result of the outsourcing process. If possible, the buyer should implement service-level measurements before outsourcing, both to obtain a baseline and to determine the adequacy of the measurement process.

The SLA should also address who is responsible for measuring service levels and how often. Depending on the type of activity being measured, service levels can be measured by the vendor, the buyer, third parties, or some combination. The time period for which the service level is measured should be long enough to be meaningful, but not so long as to be cost prohibitive or unfair to the vendor. Of significance is the fact that pricing, in the form of credits or bonuses, may be tied to achieving or failing to achieve service levels, as well as events of default. Credits can be handled through either cash rebates to the buyer or credits against future amounts owed to the vendor. Reporting and availability of compliance data should be agreed upon.

TIPS & TECHNIQUES

Avoiding a Common Mistake in Setting Service Levels

Organizations often set a standard or average service level but neglect to define appropriate levels for out-of-compliance performance.

For example, if the service level for a call center requires that 95 percent of all calls must be answered within a certain time period, the SLA should also address the minimum acceptable standard for the remaining 5 percent of the calls.

SLAs should set target service levels and minimum service levels. Deviations from target service levels can result in credits to the buyer or bonuses to the vendor, as appropriate. Failure to meet minimum service levels may result in termination of the outsourcing contract for cause.

Careful consideration should also be given to the buyer's remedies resulting from failure to meet service levels. Credits and contract termination may be appropriate responses.

Planning for Changes in Service Levels The buyer and vendor need to anticipate that service levels will change over time, whether because of changes in customer requirements, technologic advances, regulatory requirements, or improvements in the vendor's processes. Because of the specificity required in SLAs, vendors and buyers should fully discuss the change processes that will be agreed on. Both parties need to keep in mind that the touchstone for SLAs and change processes should be to align the interests of the vendor and buyer as much as possible.

Pricing

Pricing of outsourced services may be set in any number of ways, and combinations of the various pricing alternatives are common. Fixed fee, volume of transactions, and cost plus are some common examples of options used in BPO relationships. In evaluating the pricing of an outsourcing agreement, BPO buyers should be aware that certain costs relating to the management of the outsourcing relationship can never be eliminated.

The choice of fee structure for a BPO contract should be motivated primarily by the desired outcomes. Buyers and vendors must consider the fee structure of the contract because unexpected future events could lead to financially burdensome obligations. For example, a BPO contract may specify that the vendor receive compensation for every successful handling of a returned retail item. This may be workable if the retailer controls its returns and has trained its customers to return goods only if they have the receipt. However, the fee structure would become unworkable if the retailer unilaterally decided to waive the receipt requirement, leaving the vendor overwhelmed with returned goods it has no way of verifying.

Outsourcing arrangements can run from thousands to millions of dollars over the course of a multiyear agreement, depending on the size and complexity of the work. In general, contracts can be written on a fixed price or variable pricing basis. However, those are just two of the available contract pricing options (Exhibit 4.6).

EXHIBIT 4.6

BPO Pricing Models

Cost Plus

This model entails the service provider to be paid the actual costs, plus a predetermined profit percentage. This model allows very little flexibility when business objectives and technology change during the duration of the outsourcing contract. Neither does it provide any incentive for the service provider to perform more efficiently.

Unit Pricing

This model assumes a predetermined rate established by the service provider for a particular level of service. The organization pays based on its usage.

Fixed Pricing

In this model, a fixed price for the service is established for the duration of the contract. Some organizations prefer this approach, as they know exactly what the service provider's price will be, even in the future. The challenge with this approach is that the organization must adequately define the scope of the process and design effective metrics before signing the contract. If not, the impact will be the service provider claiming a particular service or service level that is beyond the scope of the contract, making the buyer liable for additional charges.

Variable Pricing

This pricing model involves the use of a fixed price at the low end of the service provider's service with variables based on higher service levels. The effectiveness of this model depends on specifically defining the scope of process and metrics.

Performance-Based Pricing

Providing incentives to motivate the service provider to perform at peak level is the main thrust of this model. For example, the organization could offer a bonus reward if a project is completed ahead of schedule or demand that the service provider pay a penalty if performance is below the satisfactory level stipulated in the contract. Performance-based model should be used to extract excellence in the delivery of the service provider.

Co-Sharing Risk/Reward

In this model, the organization and the service provider each have an amount of money at risk and each stands to gain a percentage of the profits if the service provider's performance is optimum and achieves the organization's business objectives. Outsourcing is not just about throwing everything away to the outsourcing partner to save costs. It can be a profitable relationship for both the outsourcing organization and the service provider if they were to work out the service level agreement and pricing model, as well as set the expectations from the beginning.

Term of the Contract

The term of the contract is important, especially since many companies terminate outsourcing arrangements before the end of the contract period. The term should at minimum match the life cycle of the processes involved and the changes in the business cycle. Setting the term should take into account the volatility of the outsourced service, including anticipated changes in scope, SLAs, and pricing. It should also be considered in the context of the client's right to end the contract for convenience (without cause) and of the direct and indirect costs associated with such termination, as discussed later.

Governance

Governance is the process of administering and monitoring the performance phase of the BPO life cycle to ensure that the interests of the vendor and buyer remain aligned and that the goals of the parties are met through the most efficient processes available. Stated more simply, it involves assessing performance and managing change. Depending on the size and complexity of the outsourcing relationship, governance may be implemented through single points of contact between the parties or through committees with multiple representatives of both parties.

Certain basic factors are fundamental to the success of the governance process. Communication and reporting are essential. The governance structure should address schedules of meetings and scope of authority, especially with respect to change processes involving SOW, compliance with SLA standards, and the use of benchmarking to establish new standards or pricing. Depending on the seniority of those involved in the process, escalation of disputes arising from governance may also be appropriate.

Intellectual Property

The transfer, use, disclosure, protection, and development of intellectual property (IP) are some of the most significant legal issues in the outsourcing process. When first considering an outsourcing initiative, companies should carefully assess the IP ramifications of outsourcing.[10]

IP laws and enforcement vary considerably around the world. Many countries have laws protecting IP and are signatories to the World Trade Organization's intellectual property rights provisions, which are collectively known as the Trade-Related Aspects of Intellectual Property Rights (TRIPs). However, there is a mixed track record of local enforcement of IP rights belonging to U.S. firms outsourcing offshore. Until the countries where vendors are located establish a better record of protecting these rights, BPO buyers who rely on the laws do so at their peril.[11]

Obviously, the most prudent course is to keep vital IP within the United States. If an organization does transfer IP offshore, however, it should rely heavily on self-help to protect its assets.[12] This begins with conducting thorough due diligence regarding potential vendors and their security and confidentiality procedures. It also includes understanding the culture of the vendor's country toward the IP of foreigners; it is no secret that some nations view foreign IP as communal property. There are indications that India would like to differentiate itself from these countries by providing strong legal protection for the IP of foreigners.

Industry-Specific Concerns

Depending on the nature of the outsourced process, additional regulatory hurdles may need to be addressed. For example, if the outsourced process involves health care information such as insurance claims processing, the contract should address compliance with the Health Insurance Portability and Accountability Act of 1996 (HIPAA). HIPAA requires that health care organizations establish procedures and systems to prevent unauthorized access to certain protected health information.[13] Pursuant to HIPAA, the buyer must have the right to terminate the outsourcing contract if the vendor breaches any provision of HIPAA and fails to correct the problem. Similarly, if the client is a financial institution subject to the Gramm-Leach-Bliley Act (GLB), and the outsourced process involves financial information of customers, then the contract should address compliance with GLB.[14] Under GLB, financial institutions must secure private customer data.

Termination of the Contract

In considering termination provisions, the initial focus should be to anticipate the circumstances under which BPO buyers might desire to end the outsourcing relationship. The contractual right to terminate a BPO relationship can be granted for two reasons: (1) convenience and (2) cause.

Because of the requirement for flexibility and change management in the outsourcing process, it is imperative that the buyer has the right to terminate for convenience. In most instances, vendors will be justified in requiring a fee in conjunction with termination for convenience. The amount should vary in relation to the anticipated financial position of the parties at the time of the termination.

Typically, vendors cannot terminate for convenience because of the extreme cost, risk, and disruption resulting to the buyer. If the vendor insists on allowing termination for convenience, the termination fee specified in the contract should reflect these factors. Typically, vendors can terminate only for cause, usually meaning the failure of the buyer to pay amounts owed to the vendor.

The contract should specifically define what allows the buyer to terminate for cause. Areas to be addressed include:

- Material as well as continuing or repetitive nonmaterial breaches of the outsourcing contract.

- Financial insolvency or insecurity of the service provider, including setting objective standards for financial insecurity, reporting requirements, and auditing rights.

- Retention of key employees or overall turnover rates of the vendor's workforce.

- So-called cross-default provisions with respect to the vendor's contracts with other service providers (subcontractors) that may or may not be working on the buyer's outsourced process. If the service provider is in default under these contracts, it can constitute a default under the outsourcing contract.

- Changes in control with respect to the vendor. These may result in the replacement of the management team in which the buyer placed its trust at the outset of the relationship or may result in the vendor's providing services to—or even becoming a competitor of—the buyer, with attendant risks to the buyer's IP.

- Changes of control with respect to the buyer. These may result in the divestiture of the processes being outsourced or otherwise obviate the need for outsourcing altogether. New management of the buyer may not be comfortable with outsourcing for any number of reasons, so the vendor should have the right to end the contract because of management changes.

Transition

If a BPO relationship falls apart and one or both parties decide to terminate the agreement, it may be necessary for the buyer to reabsorb the outsourced process or find another vendor. In either case, the transition of the outsourced process should be considered in the original contract.

The reasons for this are clear. Consider all of the planning and implementation entailed in outsourcing a process from a buyer to a vendor. Now imagine how much more difficult that process might be when the original buyer is no longer in control of the process and its assets and personnel. To add to the challenge, consider the fact that the transition may well be from an unhappy or incompetent vendor. Thus, the transition from one vendor to another, or the reintegration of the outsourced process back to the buyer, is exponentially more difficult than the original outsourcing process. As a result, careful consideration should be given as to how the transition may be effected, and detailed transition provisions included in the contract.

A transition plan should have a commitment by the vendor to provide transition-planning assistance. This should include inventories of hard and soft assets, copies of relevant data, detailed descriptions of procedures, and other information relevant to the outsourced process. The buyer should have the right to use this data and disclose it to other potential vendors, to purchase the assets and hire key personnel related to the outsourced process, and to assume key contracts.

Furthermore, the plan should address the need for parallel process-ing for some period of time while the process migrates to a new vendor or back to the buyer. There may also be a need for continued use of shared assets, such as computer networks. And just as aligning vendor–buyer interests is vital to a successful contract, aligning those interests during the transition is equally significant. Usually, this takes the form of monetary incentives for a successfully implemented transition.

Force Majeure

Outsourcing contracts typically include force majeure clauses, which excuse the vendor from performance in the case of natural disasters such as fire and weather-related catastrophes. In light of the geopolitical pos-tures of many of the countries where BPO vendors are located, war and terrorism are also likely triggers of force majeure clauses. However, because of the significant function that outsourced processes often play in the buyer's business, a well-crafted contract should contemplate more than just excusing the vendor from performance during the force majeure event. It should also link the triggering of a force majeure event with disaster recovery plans and business continuation plans. To the extent that a buyer cannot significantly minimize its risk in that regard, insurance should be addressed.

Dispute Resolution

The outsourcing contract is a living document that must have change management processes integrated within it. Change, however, inevitably invites disagreement, and the contract should anticipate this. The dispute resolution process begins where corporate governance ends. When all elements of the governance process have been engaged and the parties have still failed to resolve their dispute, legal processes must be pursued.

These processes can have escalation procedures built in, just like the governance process. Dispute resolution may be initiated through informal, nonbinding procedures such as mediation. Beyond these procedures, however, the dispute resolution process will progress to either binding arbitration or litigation. If the parties decide to use arbitration, they must agree on the rules. In international transactions, parties often use the rules and procedures promulgated by the International Chamber of Commerce's International Court of Arbitration;[15] in domestic transactions, they often specify that arbitration will be conducted pursuant to the Commercial Arbitration Rules of the American Arbitration Association.

In either case, questions of venue and choice of law must be addressed. Venue is the place where the dispute is to be resolved. The parties should consider questions of efficiency in terms of proximity to the persons and facilities proximate to the dispute as well as questions of neutrality. Choice-of-law provisions determine what laws will govern the interpretation of the contract and rules of the dispute, and they are usually determined by the golden rule—he who has the gold rules.

Summary

Identifying, selecting, and contracting with the right BPO vendor is essential to the success of any initiative. The selection process should be thorough and rigorous and take on a life cycle of its own that includes appointing a vendor selection team; establishing qualifications; developing an initial long list of potential vendors; distributing a request for information, followed by the RFP; evaluating the proposals; culling the list of prospective vendors; and making a final decision. In the event that no vendor satisfies the specific requirements of the RFP, the buyer should consider abandoning the BPO project rather than altering the specifications or forcing a fit.

Similar attention and consideration should go into developing the BPO contract, especially given the fact that poorly crafted contracts are a key contributor to the failure of buyer-vendor relationships. The terms of any BPO contract are numerous and far-reaching, requiring a collaborative rather than competitive approach to negotiation. In crafting the contract, both parties should pursue precise language in the spirit that both reflects the strategic nature of their relationships and provides mechanisms that anticipate and resolve future problems.

Endnotes

1. Joanne Wojcik, "Formal Process Advised in Vendor Searches," *Business Insurance* (November 16, 1998): 16.

2. Vaughan Michell and Guy Fitzgerald, "The IT Outsourcing Market-Place: Vendors and Their Selection," *Journal of Information Technology* 12 (1997): 223–237.

3. "Keys to Success: Stability of Partner, Maturity of Processes & Industry Focus," *Insurance & Technology* (August 2002): 28.

4. Charles A. Weber, John R. Current, and Anand Desai, "VendOR: A Structured Approach to Vendor Selection and Negotiation," *Journal of Business Logistics* 21, no. 1 (2000): 135–167.

5. "'Must' Provisions to Consider for Your Outsourcing Contracts," *Supplier Selection and Management Report* (October 2003): 10–12.

6. Farok J. Contractor, "A Generalized Theorem for Joint Venture and Licensing Negotiations," *Journal of International Business Studies* (Summer 1985): 23–50.

7. Mario Apicella, "Shaking Hands Is Not Enough," *InfoWorld* (April 30, 2001): 49–50.

8. Dai Davis, "Service Level Agreements: What Are They? Why Do We Need Them?" *Credit Management* (May 2002): 36.

9. Laton McCartney, "How Do You Set Up an Effective SLA?" *Inter@ctive Week* (September 27, 2000): 30.

10. Patrick Thibodeau, "Offshore Risks are Numerous, Say Those Who Craft Contracts," *Computerworld* (November 3, 2003): 12.

11. Bart Perkins, "A Reality Check on Going Offshore," *Computerworld* (June 16, 2003): 42.

12. "How to Protect IP Before Entering into New Relationships," *Supplier Selection & Management Report* (April 2003): 2–4.

13. HIPAA Compliance, ASPs, Outsourcing, and Vendor Relationships," *Medical Benefits* (July 15, 2002): 11.

14. Brad Miller, "Outsourcing Aids Compliance," *Bank Technology News* (December 2001): 52.

15. Walter Mattli, "Private Justice in a Global Economy: From Litigation to Arbitration," *International Organization* (Autumn 2001): 919–947.

CHAPTER 5

Managing BPO-Related Change

After reading this chapter, you will be able to:

- Increase the potential for executing a successful BPO transition stage strategy

- Develop an effective BPO project management plan, and determine whether the project should be managed by an individual, a few people, or a team

- Recognize five principles that guide change management and understand how they can be applied to support the transition stage of a BPO initiative

- Identify three critical skills that serve as the foundation of a successful BPO relationship

- Better determine the depth and scope of a BPO relationship, and make decisions as to whether to use the assets of the buyer or vendor and whose business culture to adopt

- Understand what constitutes—and how to develop—a trusting, successful buyer–vendor relationship

- Minimize or eliminate the factors that can threaten the success of a BPO initiative

As the BPO life cycle moves into the operational stage, organizations will find themselves facing important changes. A great deal of time and expense has gone into preparation, and at this stage it is critical to protect that investment in two key ways: (1) by recognizing and managing the risks that the BPO-induced change represents and (2) by managing the often complex relationship that exists between BPO buyers and vendors. An effective change management strategy—which should not be implemented until the BPO contract is signed and the launch date set—can identify the tactics that contribute to a smooth BPO transition. A formalized relationship management strategy can solidify the vendor–buyer foundation, ensuring that both parties respect each other's role and operate within the parameters of a well-designed project management plan.

Changes and Challenges Facing the BPO Organization

It goes without saying that any organization must assess its own unique challenges in undertaking a BPO project. At the same time, there are general issues that almost all organizations must confront, including:

- Establishing a vision of the future state of the organization
- Securing leadership as well as management of the BPO transition
- Communicating with internal staff about the BPO transition
- Managing organization culture beyond the process affected by BPO
- Managing job loss and changeover to new management
- Establishing business continuity and new performance benchmarks

To deal effectively with these issues, organizations need an overarching project management plan, an understanding of basic change management principles, and recognition of the numerous change-induced issues likely to arise. By paying attention to, and planning for, these matters early in the process, organizations can keep their BPO initiative on track.

BPO Project Management Plan

Although signed and sealed, the BPO contract does not provide the flexibility and responsiveness necessary to manage an ongoing project. That requires a second document, the project management plan, that the contract should allude to but not spell out in detail. It needs to be fluid enough to adapt as the needs and competitive conditions of each firm change, and include provisions to enable these adjustments. At the same time, it must contain basic project management details such as goals and objectives, timelines, milestones, and key term working definitions.

Individual or Team?

Developing a project management plan requires the buyer and vendor to assign a dedicated team or, at minimum, an individual (the internal BPO champion) to design the plan, manage the project on an ongoing basis,

TIPS & TECHNIQUES

Know the Roles—and the Role Players

Basically, the project management plan is designed to provide a disciplined framework of execution that ensures the BPO transition phase gives way to the operating phase.[a] However, it has another key objective as well: establishing and identifying roles and role players from each organization—buyer and vendor. These roles and role players will be responsible for project outcomes and accountable to the BPO steering team.

[a]D. Hodgson, "Disciplining the Professional: The Case of Project Management," *Journal of Management Studies* (September 2002): 803–821.

and implement changes as needed.[1] Although this adds short-term costs to the project, it will usually prove to be less costly in the long run because issues can be anticipated and managed before they become problems. In general, project management costs should not exceed 7 percent of total project costs.[2]

The decision to use an individual or team approach to project management depends on several factors. For example, since an offshore outsourcing relationship can bring a range of issues (e.g., cultural, language, time zone, etc.) not generally encountered onshore, it may require a more intensive, team-based approach. Similarly, a buyer managing multiple vendors instead of just one may have to establish numerous BPO champions or Project Management Teams to deal with each vendor. This creates a further need to integrate the various project managers to ensure they communicate and share best practices and lessons learned.[3]

However, a team-based approach can lead to problems of accountability if there are no one-to-one links between individuals and discrete project management responsibilities. That is, even when a team approach is used, individual team members should be assigned clear responsibilities for particular aspects of the project, and they should have clear reporting channels. Exhibit 5.1 highlights some of the issues to consider in deciding whether to take a team or individual approach to project management.

Hybrid Approach

A hybrid approach that can alleviate the potential for diffusion of accountability is to assign a BPO champion to develop the Project Management Team (PMT). In this method, project management responsibility remains clearly with the BPO champion, who answers to the Steering Team and is held accountable for overall project performance (Exhibit 5.2). This person is likely to have participated on the BPO Analysis Team (BAT), the vendor selection team (VST), or both, and will generally have

EXHIBIT 5.1

Factors Relevant to Choosing between a Team or Individual BPO Relationship Manager

Individual	Team
Single BPO Provider	Multiple BPO Providers
Cost reduction is primary goal	Strategic planning is primary goal
One process outsourced, with low probability of additional outsourcing	Multiple proccesses outsourced
Onshore BPO provider	Offchoro a noarohorc DPO provideɩ

EXHIBIT 5.2

BPO Project Management Team in the Overall Project Team Structure

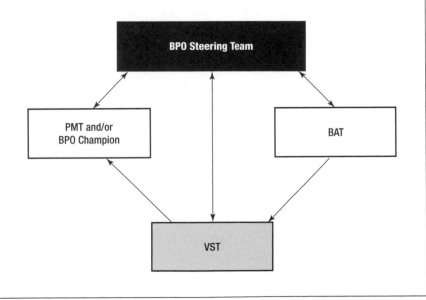

high visibility within the organization and possess skills in communications, negotiations, and business reasoning. He or she should also:

- Be able to organize and manage a team
- Be highly familiar with the business case for BPO
- Be willing and able to articulate, discuss, or defend the project

Generally speaking, the PMT should consist of members representing a range of organizational functions, including individuals from each firm, to ensure a diverse skill set that covers financial, technical, and human resource capabilities. Other roles that might be assigned to team members include:

- *Facilitator.* Responsible for setting meetings and arranging meeting locations
- *Recorder.* Responsible for taking notes during the meeting and distributing minutes to each team member
- *Liaison.* Responsible for maintaining communication between the team and other organizational units

General Principles of Change Management

The PMT is responsible for implementing the organization's change management strategy. Although much has been written about change management—and there is no consensus as to what strategy is best for a BPO initiative—one thing is certain: Well-chosen actions taken to manage change are less important than their consistent and well-communicated application.[4]

This does not mean to suggest that all managerial interventions are created equal; consistently applying a poor technique will inevitably produce poor results. That is why "well chosen" is added as a caveat. The change management strategy should be the one that makes sense *under the circumstances*. It would be difficult for the PMT to explain and/or defend its tactics if it were obvious they were inappropriate or plainly ineffective.

TIPS & TECHNIQUES

Concept of Satisficing

Most change management scholars would agree that any attempt to achieve *optimum* results is likely to lead to paralysis, as the search for the perfect technique to match current conditions would be highly time consuming and fraught with endless debate. The predominant concept today is *satisficing*—producing results that exceed certain prespecified and, hopefully, measurable para-meters, but might not be the optimum solution.[a] Satisficing is a concept not used often enough in organizational change manage-ment. It is a handy concept—handier than, say, synergy—that promotes action over inaction, results over paralysis, and consis-tency over trendy management theories. As such, it should become a part of the PMT's lexicon and a pillar of efficient change management.

[a]Sidney G. Winter, "The Satisficing Principle in Capability Learning," *Strategic Management Journal* (October/November 2000): 981–996.

In light of the recommendation that a consistent application of a well-chosen strategy, and not the strategy itself, is foremost in effective BPO-induced change management, one question naturally arises: What management principles qualify as well chosen? Experience and scholarly research generally agree that effective change management has five primary requirements:

1. Compelling vision of the outcome of the change process

2. Visible leadership from top management

3. Extensive communication and opportunities for employee feedback

4. Ability to deal with job loss and changeover

5. Ability to maintain business continuity and benchmark performance

Creating a Compelling Vision

While there continues to be debate over its role in organizational achievement, *vision* can contribute to the process of aligning goals and individual efforts. In this context, vision can bring clarity to the outcome of a challenging project, helping people establish a sense of flow and ownership that can produce superior performance under difficult circumstances.[5] As such, it is instrumental to an effective change management plan.

Power of Storytelling

An effective vision is nothing more than a tale—a story—of what the outcome of a project is expected to *look* and *feel* like to organizational members. Managers must create the vision to determine how much detail is required to tell a story compelling enough to drive high performance. For skeptical listeners, more details and analogies might be needed; for the already converted, the story may require less detail and more encouragement to step out and take action.

A good corporate story does not need dramatic characters or daring action heroes. It simply needs a word-picture of the expected outcomes and the likely impact for the people operating it. Those requirements can be met by applying five basic elements needed to make storytelling an effective technique for leading change (Exhibit 5.3).

Managing a BPO transition requires placing the project in the context of the bigger picture, including the likely future state of the organization and its people. Developing and articulating a truthful story about that future state will not eliminate every problem. However, abdicating that responsibility will undoubtedly mean the organization will experience more, and more intense, change management issues during the transition.

Leadership and Management Roles

The transition phase of the BPO Life Cycle is a true turning point. The organization is implementing changes that heretofore had only been

EXHIBIT 5.3

Elements of Effective Organizational Storytelling

- **Effective stories are context specific.** Research indicates that linking an activity or project to a company's strategic challenges improves the effectiveness of the initiative.
- **Effective stories are level appropriate.** The storyteller should frame stories so that participants can see themselves in it and reflect on what they might do to resolve the challenges it poses.
- **Role models tell effective stories.** Storytellers must be both highly respected role models and highly accessible coaches.
- **Effective stories have drama.** The best stories focus on the storyteller's need to make tough choices, usually without perfect information or complete agreement among involved parties.
- **Effective stories have high learning value.** For a story to be effective it must stimulate learning, and for learning to have impact it must produce changes in behavior.

talked about. The rumors and fears associated with the preoperational BPO phases have given way to real changes in organizational workflow, personnel, policies, and procedures. Despite their traditionally separate functions—managers spend their time on operations, leaders on vision—both are central to success at this stage. Managers are needed to help guide these new ways of doing things into the organization's overall workflow; leaders are needed to hold the organization together with steadfast vision and courage.

Managers and Their Challenges   Managers are faced with operational challenges, deadlines, and goals—yet they must motivate others to reach their goals. In BPO, it is sometimes necessary to motivate others to perform when their jobs are being eliminated and/or the threat of job elimination looms. Other impediments to a BPO implementation that must be managed include:

- Effects on personnel not displaced by the BPO project, but who may fear being next in line
- Attitudes of personnel regarding the presence of outsiders in the organization
- Attempts by some to impede progress, or a lack of willing participation in the changeover
- Fear of failure under the new workflow model

Realism, Determination, and Honesty   Managers must deal with BPO-induced change with realism and determination. Sugarcoating an obvious shift toward head-count reduction and cost containment through BPO will only fuel the rumors and anxiety. During transformational organizational change, many managers mistakenly attempt to paint a rosy picture despite overwhelming evidence to the contrary. They do this out of a natural aversion to being the bearer of bad news or, on occasion, based on denial—not wanting to believe outsourcing might target their own jobs in the future.

Honest communication about organizational goals, likely outcomes of a BPO implementation, and the steps being taken to help workers deal with the change is the best-practice technique for managers. Yet, it is often difficult to practice this approach. Some managers cannot be honest with employees because they do not know what is going to happen. That is a leadership issue that will be discussed in the next section. Even if the manager does not know the full implications of a BPO transition, it is better to communicate *that*—admitting to personal ignorance—rather than trying to provide false assurances.

Honesty and Quantity of Communications Are Critical   Right behind honesty as an important tactic for managing BPO-induced change is communication. A manager could practice honesty but still be excessively Spartan in his or her communication patterns. In the throes of dramatic organizational change, people need to talk to one another because they need to understand. A manager may not be a great communicator, but great communication is not required. What is required is communication *quantity* leavened by *honesty*.

Managers with a tendency toward introversion are not excluded. If they are uncomfortable with speeches or group meetings, there are other communication channels at their disposal: e-mails, memoranda, company newsletters, and employee portals. Managers should leverage multiple channels in communicating with employees about pending changes, what the organization is doing to help them during the change, and, most important, the rationale for the change.

Overcoming the Obstructionists   As the BPO transition unfolds, managers will encounter individuals who will attempt to obstruct the project either overtly or covertly. Overt obstructionists are fairly easy to handle. They are vocal and readily identify themselves as opponents, and can be managed directly using common disciplinary and motivational tactics.

Covert obstructionists are more insidious, however. They oppose change but work quietly to obstruct it. They can engage in direct sabotage, but are usually more cunning. They impede progress by omission, rather than commission, withholding key information or data they know would aid the transition—and not offering it unless directly asked. They appear to be contributing and happy; in fact, they are happy only in their subversion.

Identifying Covert Obstructionists   Covert obstructionists can be dealt with, but they have to be rooted out first. Although they are unlikely to identify themselves, they can be uncovered, but only with help from those working on the transition. Managers must actively query

Making Change Work

In November 1999, New York-Presbyterian Hospital (NYPH) announced a seven-year, $228 million information technology (IT) *outsourcing* contract with First Consulting Group (FCG). The contract created a third entity, FCG *Management* Services, to perform the work—a step that included the hiring of more than 400 NYPH staff into the new unit.

NYPH wanted immediate benefits from the predictable costs, service levels, and outcomes offered by *outsourcing*. "The biggest issue a CIO faces after signing the contract is managing the performance objectives for the first six months," said Diane Daniele, interim CIO for NYPH.

NYPH's office of the chief information officer (OCIO) designed a governance model to make IT a more effective investment tool by focusing on strategic planning and thinking, monitoring, governing partnerships, and *change management*. The OCIO is a champion of IT *change* at the hospital. "You must show people what the future looks like and restructure the business simultaneously," said Guy Scalzi, NYPH's former CIO and now account manager for the New York outsource team.

The trench work of transition and *change management* continues each day at NYPH with core process improvement teams focused on everything from leadership training to wiring closet inspections. Sharing leadership roles with the OCIO speeds up integration as well.

Change in how people communicate is another benefit of outsourcing. Scalzi put high-potential managers into the applications areas and told them to break down the runtime performance barriers and open up the client communication channels. The outsourcing culture rewards leaders who collaborate and communicate and does not reward the information blockers, Daniele said.

Although they were initially skeptical about the outsourcing agreement's impact on service and loss of control, physicians, too, have experienced positive changes.

Source: Adapted from Bob Smith, "Outsourcing on a Grand Scale," *Health Management Technology* (July 2000): 18–20.

others to determine if there has been any unnecessary foot-dragging or apparent lack of motivation assisting the transition. This should be done in a matter-of-fact rather than an accusatory manner, and managers should be careful not to impugn anyone who is working diligently to help the process along.

Covert obstructionists are identified through behavior patterns rather than direct acts or verbalizations. As the manager queries various individuals involved in the transition about how easy they are finding it to get what they need and where the bottlenecks seem to be, covert obstruction will reveal itself. It will be exposed in a recurrent pattern of tardiness or sloppiness in deliverables. Covert obstructionists will deliver what they are asked, but it will usually be less than professional grade and often delayed.

Leadership: Visible, Accessible, Articulate   Leadership throughout the BPO transition must be visible and accessible. Transition leaders (as opposed to managers) are expected to have a firm grasp of the BPO business case and an ability to articulate it. Furthermore, they should have a *granular* grasp

TIPS & TECHNIQUES

Managing Obstructionists

After obstructionists are confronted, they must be controlled. The best way to accomplish that is through direct management.

Managers must be involved with detailing the expected deliverables and time frame in the transition, which must then be linked to the covert obstructionist's regular performance review process. It is often advantageous to "out" them, then provide clear and unambiguous expectations of future performance.

Of course, managers must follow up on these expectations and be prepared to use disciplinary tactics if the performance objectives are not being met.

of the business case; that is, they should be able to link it to organizational units and the individuals who work in those units. Above all, leaders must be able to answer the inevitable question "What's in it for me?"

Companies undertaking BPO projects often have experience with transformational change. In that regard, many within these organizations have been through restructuring initiatives and may have developed a level of maturity with managing change of that magnitude. In organizations like this, leaders are called on to inject new enthusiasm into the organizational *zeitgeist*. Expressions of better possible futures for the company and its employees are the preferred strategy. Occasionally, leaders shield themselves from negative reactions by asserting that the BPO decision is a matter of organizational survival in a highly competitive economy—a decision beyond anyone's control. Although that may be true, it has the ring of cowardice. It is better to describe the BPO strategy as a carefully laid plan that stands to generate compelling advantages for the organization and its employees. Leaders cannot shrink from the need to articulate a vision during times of transformational change[6] and to help people paint a mental picture of a future that will be better and more satisfying than the present.[7]

Communicating with Employees

Effective employee communication is vital to the BPO transition. Organizational space abhors a communication vacuum. If the space is not filled with deliberate, optimistic, and directive messages from leadership, it will be filled by rumors, gossip, and speculation from employees. People need to understand their environment and will settle for half-baked speculative explanations if no better alternatives are available.

Honesty and Sophisticated Honesty   Effective employee communication begins with a simple notion: honesty. Honesty is the best policy not only because it is ethically correct, but also because half-truths and lies will

148

ultimately destroy morale and productivity. At the same time, blunt honesty is rarely a useful strategy in organizational life. It should be tempered with tact and sophistication. But beware of equivocation—perceived or otherwise. For example, organizations seeking to undertake a BPO initiative will often entertain a head-count reduction. Communicating that reality to employees could well be detrimental to productivity. At the same time, evading, denying, or waffling over the issue would be disingenuous and obvious even to those unskilled at reading social cues.

So the key to effective employee communication is not simply honesty, but *sophisticated* honesty, and requires managers to deliver messages in two ways:

1. *Accurately*. This pertains to the truthfulness of the communication. The rule is simple: Do not lie.
2. *Competently*. This relates to the detail the communication provides. Employees at different levels need different levels of detail about the project.

At minimum, managers should communicate what the BPO initiative means to employees personally and what the organization intends to do to help them through the transition.[8] Every impact message from management should be accompanied by a "Here's what we're going to do about it" message. This may even include an explanation of the outplacement support for employees who could lose their jobs.

Managing Culture Beyond the Outsourced Process

Beyond the organizational units immediately affected by the BPO project are employees who are friends, relatives, and acquaintances of those affected. BPO project managers must not overlook the ripple effects created by outsourcing and the threat others might feel from seeing the impact of BPO on their colleagues. Compounding this will be concerns about workflow issues and day-to-day business continuity. Organizational units that work closely with the outsourced function may worry about the ability of the vendor to achieve the same level of productivity. Other concerns include:

- Will we have to work extra hard to make the BPO transition work?

- Will my job change because new work processes are introduced?

- Who will receive my work output, and will he or she understand it?

- Will I be able to adapt to the vendor and its people?

- How will the organization's customers react to changes in personnel and/or procedures?

As part of this responsibility, managers must be able to demonstrate buy-in to the BPO project and refrain from public nay-saying if they do not fully support the initiative. Thus, top leadership must build BPO support across organizational boundaries—horizontally and vertically. At the very least, the management team must be united in its public support of the initiative. Optimally, everyone should be aligned to back the project and be mobilized to assist as needed.

Managing Job Loss and Changeover

Managing job loss and changeover is among the hardest challenges managers face. Most rank-and-file employees who will likely be displaced by a BPO initiative are living paycheck to paycheck, and they probably will not greet the organizational decision to outsource with shouts of joy. Whether the anticipated job displacement includes termination or shifting responsibilities, the reaction is predictable: Some will rush for the exit; some will cower and hope for the best; some will fight; some will simply deny reality. Each of these reactions must be managed. The good news is, they can.

Detailed Reduction-in-Force Plan   A thorough analysis of BPO project costs will include projected job losses and job shifts, and expenses related to outplacement and/or retraining services. Although many firms opt for a ruthless strategy during reduction-in-force (RIF) initiatives, others have found value in a more humane approach. But regardless of the approach, a detailed RIF plan is essential to minimize rancor, control the culture, and reduce liability exposure.[9]

A detailed RIF plan will consider a wide range of factors when identifying who will be terminated and the procedures for undertaking the terminations. It should consider each individual's skills and determinations of their relative contributions to the firm. Simply using an across-the-board RIF strategy is unwise if it risks the termination of promising up-and-comers. RIF plans are typically developed by the management team in an off-site and secure setting. The list of individuals to be terminated should be carefully guarded, and managers should receive thorough training on procedures that will be used with the terminated employees.

TIPS & TECHNIQUES

Elements of a Defensible RIF Plan

Employers should follow these essential steps when carrying out a reduction in force:

- Decide what criteria will be used to select those for termination (e.g., geography, seniority, line of work, merit ranking).
- Make sure the criteria are followed.
- Be certain that the RIF criteria conform to company policy.
- Have at least one level of review of termination decisions.
- Perform a "disparate impact" review of those chosen for termination to make sure there is no discrimination, even unintentional.
- Document the entire process.

Source: Fair Employment Practices Guidelines (Aspen Publishers, January 15, 2003).

Reducing the Impact on Displaced Employees The RIF plan should also consider options for reducing the impact of the displacement for employees. For example, early retirement programs may be an option for senior employees. Voluntary buyouts of employment agreements may be used in cases in which a contract is in force. Many organizations attempt to obtain a release of potential claims from workers terminated as a result of an RIF. This requires some form of consideration from the organization, usually severance pay. Other forms of consideration include a reference letter or payment of insurance premiums for a defined period.[10] Some firms have been able to shift employees from direct employment to contract labor, using them on an as-needed basis, an arrangement that often works well for the organization and the worker.

The RIF plan should include provisions for helping displaced employees get another job. Some firms set up career and psychological counseling services to help employees through the initial shock. Many also establish job centers—usually away from the corporate campus—that provide job listings and support in resume writing and interviewing skills. Among the other short-term services firms can provide are day care for parents who cannot afford it without a job, seminars on job hunting, and training programs to help provide new skills for a changed job market.

Business Continuity and Benchmarking

It is to be expected that performance indicators for the outsourced process are likely to be down or flat during the early stages of the transition. Also, processes that are tightly linked to the outsourced process will potentially experience difficulties during this phase. Despite these expected dips, managers should have detailed benchmarks that provide a means of judging the extent of the performance downturn and helping determine if intervention is required.

Business continuity during transformational change is difficult, often requiring long hours and skill-stretching behavior. Managers annoyed by frequent employee meetings and communication will be challenged to participate in these areas. The organization may need to work carefully with local media representatives, who are always looking for a human-interest story amidst the outsourcing-induced RIF. Public relations and corporate communications may be called upon to assertively address challenging questions about global job shifts and free trade.

Business continuity requires the organization to manage internal disruptions to workflow by establishing acceptable limits on performance variation. Six Sigma goals may need to be relaxed slightly during the BPO transition to account for the necessary learning curve. Yet, the organization does not merely want *any* result to count as acceptable. Reasonable, transition-phase-only benchmarks should be adopted and monitored. Managers should be ready to intervene when performance falls below the benchmark, but should be vigilant in staying the course and allowing employees to learn and improve the new system. Performance levels should rise as the transition unfolds, and new performance peaks are more likely to be sustained if managers allow the learning process to run its course.

Change and the Buyer–Vendor Relationship

BPO-induced change does not end with the impact on employees and other affected vertical and horizontal audiences, however. Once the contract is signed, the organization will find itself in a new relationship—with the BPO vendor—that will inevitably compel some degree of organizational change. While this relationship is full of potential, it is also fraught with risk. As such, companies considering BPO must understand that the traditional tactics for managing the buyer–supplier relationship are inadequate for managing a BPO relationship. So BPO buyers should be prepared to change their approaches accordingly and adopt a formal approach to BPO relationship management.

A Relationship Rooted in Key Skills   The foundation of a BPO relationship is laid when a company begins to communicate its intention to outsource. Successful management of the outsourcing relationship depends on how the requirements are defined, the objectives described, the vendor chosen, and the contract written. Additionally, the people selected to manage the relationship are key, because managing BPO relationships requires a variety of skills, including[11]:

- *Negotiation.* There will often be give and take in a BPO relationship, so it is important that the Project Management Team be skilled in negotiating points of view and in presenting them acceptably to the vendor.
- *Communication.* Outsourcing project management teams are the glue between a company's business needs and the vendor's services. Effective communication skills prevent simple problems from becoming complex ones.
- *Business knowledge.* It is important to continually understand the changing business needs and align the services from the vendor with the business objectives of the BPO buyer.

The buyer's senior management must be involved in periodically monitoring the BPO relationship and in ensuring that it stays on track. Additionally, senior management plays a critical role in communicating the reasons for and results of outsourcing across the company. To facilitate this, some firms have actually created the position of outsourcing relationship manager.

Ultimately, the barometer of a good BPO relationship is the ability of both parties to respect each other's roles and responsibilities and to operate within the confines of a mature, communicative, and trusting project management plan. The legal framework of a BPO project, while

IN THE REAL WORLD

FMC Designates an Outsourcing Relationship Manager

It is near the end of the workday on July 3, a few hours before the long Fourth of July weekend, and Jill Fosmire is fully engaged in her most serious crisis since taking her job nine months before.

FMC Corporation, a $2 billion Philadelphia-based chemical company, outsources its global wide area network and telecommunications to Plano, Texas–based Electronic Data Systems Corporation (EDS), which relies on the communications networks of now-bankrupt World-Com Inc. Her biggest question is, Will WorldCom's communications systems fail? If so, what then? Fosmire asks EDS for a contingency plan, and her own team sketches out alternatives.

In this newly created position of manager of IT *outsourcing* and contracts, Fosmire's job is to handle outsourcing crises such as these, as well as daily communication with service providers. A 20-year IT and business veteran, she's part marriage counselor, part quality-control maven, part salesperson, and exactly what FMC needed to keep its four IT outsourcing relationships focused on business results.

Outsourcing relationship manager positions are on the rise as outsourcing agreements become more complex and business environments more unpredictable. This has created a serious need for seasoned negotiators on the enterprise side who have a combination of IT experience, business savvy, sales ability, problem-solving skills, and a tight relationship with executives.

Source: Excerpted from Stacy Collett, "Wanted: Outsourcing Relationship Managers," *Computerworld* (August 12, 2002): 35.

important, is not sufficient to extract the benefits that it potentially can deliver. To achieve those benefits, vendors and buyers must trust each other, talk to each other, share with each other, and understand each other.

Fundamental Characteristics of the BPO Project

It is important to understand the four fundamental characteristics that shape any BPO relationship, regardless of industry or BPO type:[12]

- The depth of the relationship
- The scope of the relationship
- The choice of assets to use
- The choice of business culture to adopt and exploit

Depth of the Relationship

The depth of the BPO relationship depends on the criticality of the outsourced business process. The closer the outsourced process is to the core process of the buyer, the greater the depth needed in the relationship. Based on the importance of the outsourced functions and how these functions would change or evolve, the resulting relationships can be:

- *Arm's-length*, and primarily driven by cost or service-level agreement (SLA)
- *Cooperative*, necessitating intense dialogue between the parties
- *An extension of the buyer's organization*, with a number of dependencies and commitments between the parties for each other's success

As a rule of thumb, the deeper the BPO relationship, the more tightly coupled and potentially synergistic the buyer and vendor tend to be. From an operational perspective, tight coupling refers to the extent and frequency of information and resource sharing between the two firms. Deep relationships require tight coupling because the outsourced process is usually proximate to the buyer's core competence and is highly fault intolerant. Information must flow freely in both directions to ensure that the outsourced process is being executed to specification and that any variations are kept within tolerable performance limits.

A deep BPO relationship also requires the parties to develop a project management plan that specifies regular, transparent interorganizational communication and information sharing. This should include provisions for routine contacts as well as emergency meetings and communication channels. A BPO relationship that is not considered to be deep will require less frequent communications. The Project Management Team (PMT) will need to determine what is appropriate based on its shared expectations and beliefs about the nature of the relationship.

Scope of Relationship

The scope of a BPO relationship depends on whether the buyer works with separate vendors for various outsourced functions or develops a relationship with a few or just one. Working with multiple vendors for multiple functions will necessitate a larger PMT—or perhaps more than one—and poses advantages and disadvantages for buyers.

Single-service providers often have developed levels of specialization and expertise that enable them to deliver world-class service. The downside is that each outsourced process requires getting to know and manage each new vendor. Managing multiple vendors presents a multitude of challenges for the BPO buyer and adds to the overall costs of outsourcing.

Multiple-service vendors provide enhanced opportunities for strategic gains based on level of familiarity with the buyer. The more processes, information, and knowledge shared between BPO buyer and vendor, the greater the potential for insights into overall business processes and strategy. New ideas and ways of operating can and should be derived from a working relationship of this type. Whereas a downside of working with a single or limited number of vendors is that there is greater risk to the business, this can be mitigated by the level of familiarity, comfort, and confidence that would necessarily precede any decision to continue shifting processes to the multiple-service vendor.

In a multiple-vendor strategy, the project management plan may need multiple internal BPO champions. If so, the Steering Team will have to integrate the various internal teams to enable cross-functional knowledge sharing. Companies that opt for a single or limited number of vendors may be able to assign each to a single champion or PMT. In that case, the Steering Team's role is primarily oversight.

Choice of Assets

Outsourcing usually involves handing over the control and maintenance of certain processes to a third party. So the issue arises of whose assets (i.e., people, physical infrastructure, technical, etc.) will be used to execute the deal. There is no simple solution. However, the solution is made easier by focusing on business-specific issues. For example, germane to this question is the relative ease with which the buyer or vendor can obtain and manage the required assets. Another relevant factor is which firm can better invest in asset development, both for scale and innovation purposes.

Choice of Business Culture

The choice of which organization's culture and operating style to choose should be practical. There is no need to take political stands, nor should either party insist on adopting one or the other culture based on personal familiarity and comfort. The latter issue will be particularly important in offshore BPO, where cultural issues are most likely to arise. Of course, no BPO buyer or vendor should violate laws or their own ethical standards when working with an offshore (or onshore, for that matter) partner. At the same time, there will be occasions when insisting on imposing one's own culture and way of working will be counterproductive.

The watchword when choosing whose culture to leverage for the BPO project is *pragmatic*: Which culture will be most likely to lead to a successful project? This question is not easy to answer, but several key considerations can be weighed and evaluated (Exhibit 5.4).

EXHIBIT 5.4

Weighted Culture Selection Framework

Cultural Consideration	Weight
Individuals working with the outsourced processes are primarily from buyer or vendor.	.05
Culture that is closer to that of buyer's clients.	.10
Culture that is most likely to assimilate the other without major difficulty.	.15
Culture that is most likely to be able to adapt to the buyer's competitive challenges.	.20
Culture that will provide long-term-stability.	.50

BPO buyers should work closely with vendors to address the "whose culture?" issue. This is no time to shrink from asking the tough questions. A solid BPO relationship must deal frankly with cultural differences and must focus on the common goal—effective performance of the business process. Of course, a BPO buyer must always be concerned about the consequences at home from its vendor selection. Historically, a primary issue of contention has revolved around unacceptable foreign labor laws. However, the issue has now heated up politically around the issue of moving jobs outside the United States.

BPO Relationship Success Factors

The project management plan is intimately related—but not confined—to the contract between the parties. It includes elements of interpersonal and interorganizational interaction that simply cannot be specified in a contract. For example, in order for strategic benefits to be realized through BPO, the parties must develop trust in each other to understand and seek to advance their respective core business competencies. So each must reach beyond the concrete terms and conditions in the contract and SLAs, and strive to understand the competitive conditions under which the other must operate, excel, and remain profitable.

Importance and Value of Trust

Trust in the BPO context has many ingredients (Exhibit 5.5), but it is absolutely essential if the partners to the relationship are to realize gains beyond those articulated in the contract. A trusting relationship may lead to interorganizational transactions and to new, unexpected revenue opportunities that may not be included in the scope of the original contract. In fact, a dynamic BPO relationship will constantly seek ways to extend and deepen the working relationship for mutual strategic gains.

Unlike the traditional buyer–supplier relationship, the BPO relationship must be meticulously planned and managed from day one with

---

EXHIBIT 5.5

Ingredients of a Trusting BPO Relationship

- Shared vision and expectations
- Consistency of actions
- Predictability of responses
- Respectful of confidentiality issues
- Long-term, mature, and enduring
- Aligned interests and goals
- Mutual respect and understanding
- Proactive and intense communication
- Integrated systems and processes
- Encouraging and participative
- Sharing of risks and rewards
- Operating as extended organizations

strategic intent. That is, the project management plan should be designed to manage the project and achieve its basic goals, while seeking strategic gains for both buyer and vendor.

Common Factors in Successful Relationships

It is generally accepted that the tactics to effectively manage outsourcing relationships vary as widely as the relationships themselves. At the same time, however, an examination of hundreds of BPO cases also reveals that successful buyer–vendor relationships have certain factors in common:

- *The buyer must understand and respect the vendor's need to make a profit.* The relationship cannot be driven by cost reduction above all other considerations. For the vendor to continue to be motivated to provide high-quality services, there must be profit in the relationship.

- *The contract should have provisions for SLA recalibration.* As business conditions change, the original SLAs may be out of line with industry practice and need to be recalibrated.

- *The buyer's responsibilities should be clearly articulated.* Many BPO contracts clearly articulate the vendor's responsibilities, but ignore or minimize the buyer's.

- *The BPO project management plan should include provisions for changing the PMT structure or members.* Although changes in PMT structure and membership should not be cavalier, allowances should be made for member attrition and rotation.

- *The PMT should use systematic problem identification and resolution techniques.* Rather than waiting for problems to arise, the PMT should use a systematic and proactive approach based on interorganizational trust and honesty.

- *The PMT should develop interpersonal relationship norms.* These should arise from within the group and govern the manner in which PMT members relate to one another.

Profits and the BPO Relationship

A reasonable profit margin for the vendor is essential to the long-term success of an outsourcing relationship. Neither party should aspire to an unrealistic business advantage.[13] Outsourcing is designed to deliver financial benefits to the BPO buyer, to be sure, but it must also be kept in mind that the vendor is a business and must profit as well. The profit and reward that accompanies outstanding work motivates the vendor to commit resources, ensure quality and service levels, identify opportunities, address the buyer's business issues in a timely and proactive manner, and innovate.

Relationships that focus exclusively on cost reduction often lead the vendor to deliver minimum service in order to justify the continuation of the contract. This can be avoided, and both parties can reap benefits, if the buyer expects a fair profit for the vendor and encourages reinvestment of profits in extension of the vendor's core competencies. This, in turn, will enable the vendor to commit more high-level services to the buyer.

Recalibration of Terms

SLA recalibration clauses are effective tools for reassessing and adjusting contract terms.[14] Incorporating and exercising a benchmarking clause in the contractual framework of a BPO relationship provides an opportunity to baseline service levels, repair a strained relationship, and adjust terms as new business or service conditions require. By identifying and quantifying the specific elements of service delivery that need recalibration, the parties can stay motivated by virtue of the tenor of the contract. The project management framework should incorporate any contractual clauses regarding changes to SLAs and should execute changes as required. This is not as easy as it sounds. Each change will require negotiations and a thorough review of the implications. The PMT should handle all changes according to its operating principles, which may include voting guidelines and issue resolution protocols.

Buyer's Responsibilities

The BPO buyer's responsibilities to manage the outsourcing partner are one of the most neglected areas of outsourcing relationship governance. Companies tend to minimize the internal resources required to effectively manage a vendor. BPO buyers either devote too few resources to managing the vendor relationship or deploy supervisory resources that lack the skills, training, and inclination to make the relationship succeed. Relationship management becomes especially difficult if the buyer views outsourcing as an opportunity to reduce costs and cut head count. The tendency to draw PMT members only from the affected process can also be problematic. Although people from the process area may be technically qualified, they may lack the other skills needed to effectively manage the process. Attention must therefore be paid to the nontechnical skills of individuals on the PMT as well.

Changes in the Project Management Team

In a strained BPO relationship, the existence of ill will on one or both sides often presents a major hurdle to a successful resurrection of the relationship. In some cases, it may be useful to replace team members who have become hostile to the project or who have developed personal animosities. But sometimes an occasional turnover in members just makes good business sense. Changing or rotating members—except for the BPO champion—can help prevent interpersonal conflicts from developing into larger problems. It may also bring in fresh perspectives and improve the possibilities of revitalizing the relationship.

Systematic Problem Identification and Resolution

Several tools are available to the PMT to constantly monitor and assess the results of the BPO project. The metrics specified in the SLAs are a starting point. Beyond that, the team should regularly scout the external environment to determine whether strategic advantages are

Top 10 Issues Approach

If an outsourcing relationship has become damaged or strained, the PMT may want to use the Top 10 Issues strategy. It works like this: At each meeting, the PMT identifies the top 10 issues confronting the project. Subsequent meetings track the progress on the issues and, hopefully, drive them down the list and out of the top 10.

This requires significant due diligence to establish that the concerns are objective and can be unambiguously documented. Once both sides agree on the nature and extent of the issues, they are given time to develop and implement solutions to each one. The PMT's responsibility is to establish monitoring mechanisms to ensure that the buyer's or vendor's actions agreed to for each issue are actually implemented.

also accruing to the partners as a result of their BPO-based working relationship.

Many BPO partnerships have adopted the balanced scorecard approach to evaluate performance and facilitate discussion on value creation opportunities. By using added value as a scorecard perspective, the model provides the vendor with an opportunity to identify the value that is provided over the course of the contractual term and to define the linkages between business needs and services delivered.

Develop Interpersonal Relationships

There is no avoiding the necessity for buyer and vendor to develop trusting interpersonal relationships, and each can take a number of steps to foster a strong and lasting partnership (Exhibit 5.6). However, the most important factor in the interpersonal arena is the establishment of acceptable norms that govern the relationship between the parties.

EXHIBIT 5.6

Tips for Developing Effective Interpersonal BPO Relationships

- Develop an approach for the relationship as allies.
- Regard attendance at the regularly scheduled PMT meetings as a top priority.
- Be tolerant of cultural differences as they apply to issues of power and authority.
- Arrange seating during PMT meetings in a manner that avoids furthering an "us versus them" mentality.
- Seek "win-win" in negotiations over SLA term changes or contract extensions.
- Develop an understanding of and appreciation for the other party's business and competitive arena.
- Hold meetings at each other's premises on a rotating basis, allowing each to serve as the "host."

Dimensions of a Healthy Relationship

The norms of behavior in a healthy BPO relationship are based on three dimensions:[15]

1. *Flexibility.* Defines a bilateral expectation of the willingness to adapt as circumstances change.
2. *Information exchange.* Defines a bilateral expectation that buyer and vendor will proactively provide information useful to each other.
3. *Solidarity.* Defines a bilateral expectation that a high value is placed on the relationship and prescribes behaviors directed specifically toward relationship maintenance.

As PMT members interact and become comfortable with one another, norms of behavior will develop. A big mistake in managing teams is to intervene with prescribed norms, circumventing the natural group norming process. Enabling the PMT to meet often during the early stages facilitates the norming process. The PMT should attempt to codify some of its norms into its project management plan, being cognizant that the norms may need to be changed and rewritten from time to time as the team matures.

Relationship Risk Factors

It is impossible to control the way the BPO market will evolve. However, organizations can control with whom they partner and how that relationship develops, in the process minimizing the potential for negative and potentially irreparable consequences. There is ample experience among BPO buyers and vendors to highlight some of the more common pitfalls of failed relationships. Seven such pitfalls have been identified:

- Lack of appropriate buyer control
- Cultural differences
- Inflexibility in BPO agreements
- Inadequate SLA specifications and/or metrics
- Inadequate governance
- Lack of goal alignment
- Lack of integration

Lack of Appropriate Buyer Control

Organizations that undertake a BPO initiative must recognize that outsourcing is not the same as abdication. When an activity is outsourced, the buyer should dedicate a manager (BPO champion) or team (PMT) to interact with the vendor. This relationship works best when both sides seek to provide value-added service to their respective operations and strategy. However, a buyer that tries to completely control the outsourced process will undermine the leverage the vendor can employ to deliver satisfactory services.

The danger in an outsourcing relationship lies in the inability of the buyer to develop an appropriate level of control. An "appropriate" level allows the vendor the freedom to provide services without ceding the ability to prevent small problems from becoming large ones. This is a delicate balancing act that will need to be adjusted over time. For example, at the beginning of the relationship, the vendor is focused on performing at a high level and pleasing the buyer. At this point, the buyer may not need as much control as it will later in the relationship, when the enthusiasm wanes and performance becomes routine. Problems are most likely to arise when the vendor unconsciously shifts to viewing its performance as routine and reduces the level of internal oversight. A proactive relationship management approach will anticipate these fluctuations and establish metrics and reporting regimes to counteract them.

Cultural Differences

Misunderstanding and mistrust can arise when a BPO buyer initiates a project with a vendor whose organizational culture and operating style are vastly different from its own. Such differences can and often are bridged. But what matters is whether the two firms recognize the differences and

 TIPS & TECHNIQUES

Two Ways to Spot a Problem Vendor

It is a near certainty that cultural differences will be exacerbated if one or both parties are unable to listen to and understand the other. This problem can be avoided—or at least mitigated—during the vendor selection process. As the process unfolds, BPO buyers should be especially sensitive to how well bidders listen to their needs and whether the prospective vendors ask questions that reveal an awareness of potential problems arising from cultural differences. Any vendor that does not listen well or ask the right questions should probably be eliminated from consideration.

take proactive steps to deal with them. Of course, it is impossible to uncover all cultural differences during vendor selection; some will only become manifest in the operating phase. The project management plan should include inducements for each side to identify and detect problems that are a direct result of cultural differences.

Inflexibility in BPO Agreements

BPO agreements must be designed to provide for adequate flexibility in order to withstand changes in the business environment and the pressures inherent to such a contractual agreement. Typically, contract agreements are crafted on certain key assumptions pertaining to technologies, business conditions, personnel, and other relevant issues. But these assumptions will likely change with time. No matter how detailed the contract or favorable the terms, BPO agreements cannot anticipate all of the changes that occur in a dynamic, global business environment. The inability to foresee changes tends to ensure that one, if not both, of the parties will become disenchanted with the relationship over time. Long-term contracts that lack flexibility increase the likelihood of dissatisfaction between the parties and can adversely affect the relationship.

Once the contract is in force, both parties may be tempted to sub-optimize the relationship and attempt to better their lot—often at the expense of the other party. The best way to avoid this is to craft a contract for a long-term relationship with short-term SLAs that can be adjusted to meet changing conditions. The long-term provisions spell out the spirit and intent of the parties; the short-term SLAs can be altered to include changing metrics and measurement instruments, as well as changing strategic goals of one or both parties.

Inadequate SLA Specifications

SLA specifications and metrics measure the provider's performance during the operating phase of the BPO Life Cycle. They must be clearly defined and effectively designed into the contract. This allows the buyer a comfort level in turning over control of its business processes to the vendor and assures the vendor will deliver services that conform to expectations. Carefully structured SLAs and metrics can also minimize the potential that arbitrary impediments to vendor performance levels (e.g., employees who do not perform as required) do not produce adverse consequences.

Inadequate Governance

Although compliance to service levels receives adequate contractual attention, the governance structure necessary to achieve relationship maturity is too often ignored. To mitigate potential problems, the PMT should recognize and perform two main roles in the governance process:

1. *Judicial.* PMT specifies how often the parties will share information and measure performance, and what will be done in the event of nonperformance.
2. *Legislative.* PMT develops and deliberates changes to the project management plan and SLAs.

Lack of Goal Alignment

An outsourcing relationship is bound to fail when the parties do not align goals, objectives, and interests. Goal alignment means that both parties take action, including investment of time and financial resources, toward the goals they articulate to one another. Merely stating goals is not enough. Both firms must demonstrate commitment to their achievement through actions.

When one party feels the other is not living up to its stated goals, resentment and other negative emotions can arise and lead to distrust and a crumbling of the relationship. A strong project management plan will require each party not only to articulate its organizational goals and objectives, but also to show how it is pursuing them. Regularly updating each other on goal attainment and aspirations for the future is a strong antidote to the fear and mistrust that can evolve from uncertainty about the other party's commitment to the relationship.

Lack of Integration

The development of an effective BPO relationship requires not only integration of IT but also cultural replication and a sharing of vision and values. IT integration will carry its own issues—especially if the process is to be outsourced offshore—but still poses the same challenges that are central to any major software installation or hardware changeover. However, most vendors are prepared for these challenges based on their experience, and BPO buyers should leverage the market pressures that force integration responsibilities and costs primarily onto vendors. Additionally, third-party firms that specialize in getting disparate databases to talk to one another can be hired. Again, the buyer should seek to shift the integration cost burden to the vendor.

Integrating cultures, work styles, and policies and procedures is a less specific science and will pose challenges for buyers and vendors. The process of transitioning from one cultural style to another requires change management tactics covered earlier in this chapter. But the point to remember is this: Cultural organization is often overlooked, and that oversight is a leading cause of failure.

Summary

Change is intrinsic to the BPO transition stage. It presents organizations with opportunities that must be maximized and risks that must be avoided. As such, the transition must be carefully managed through a far-reaching project management plan and a strategy that respects the roles of leadership and management; the need for honest communication with employees; a recognition of the indirect impact BPO can have on non-affected business processes; an appreciation of the lingering fears and concerns that can occur during job loss and management changes; and the value of establishing and maintaining business continuity.

The impact of these changes is further complicated by the arrival of a new relationship between BPO buyers and vendors. Like the transition itself, this must be carefully managed, and can be mastered only through an ongoing focus on business benefits expected by both parties. This requires negotiation, communication, and business skills, and must be characterized by trust and the alignment of values. By understanding and pursuing the fundamental traits of a successful BPO relationship, buyers and vendors can make the critical decisions necessary to achieving project success and, potentially, forge partnerships that outlast the current initiative.

Endnotes

1. Alexa Jaworski, "Fund Managers Share Outsourcing Strategies: Communications Key," *Operations Management* (October 27, 2003): 6.

2. "Clients to Blame for Outsourcing Failure," *Global Computing Services* (June 27, 2003): 4–5.

3. "Enterprises Cannot Manage Multiple Outsourcing Vendors," *Computergram Weekly* (September 4, 2003): 4.

4. "Most Change Management Projects Fail," *Accountancy* (January 2003): 26.

5. Mihaly Csikszentmihalyi, *Flow: The Psychology of Optimal Experience* (New York: Harper & Row, 1990).

6. Roger Gill, "Change Management—Or Change Leadership?" *Journal of Change Management* (May 2003): 307–318.

7. Randy G. Pennington, "Making Changes," *Executive Excellence* (June 2000): 11.

8. Kari Reinhardt, "Communicating During Times of Change," *HRProfessional* (February/March 2001): 28–32.

9. Roger T. Sobkowiak, "Lean, Not Mean: RIF Management at The Hartford," *Information Strategy: The Executive's Journal* (Winter 1990): 19–21.

10. Gerald L. Maatman, Jr., "Management Guide on Structuring and Implementing Reductions in Force to Comply with Federal, State and Local Laws," *Labor Law Journal* (Winter 2001): 199–218.

11. Monika Rola, "Secrets to Successful Outsourcing Arrangements," *Computing Canada* (November 29, 2002): 11.

12. These fundamental characteristics have been cited widely in the literature. The authors acknowledge Accenture's White Paper "Business Process Outsourcing Big Bang," by Jane Linder, Susan Cantrell, and Scott Crist, as an influential source for this discussion.

13. Sean Doherty, "Let's Make a Deal," *Network Computing* (April 15, 2002): 52–56.

14. "Flexibility the Key to Outsourcing Success," *Global Computing Services* (May 17, 2002): 3–4.

15. Thomas Kern and Keith Blois, "Norm Development in Outsourcing Relationships," *Journal of Information Technology* 17 (2002): 33–42.

CHAPTER 6

Infrastructure Considerations and Challenges

After reading this chapter, you will be able to:

- Determine whether to use the BPO vendor's or buyer's hardware systems or whether the buyer organization should build its own

- Better ensure hardware and software compatibility between vendor and buyer infrastructures

- Conduct an infrastructure and architecture audit

- Assure that critical data and organizational knowledge are not lost during the operating phase of the BPO Life Cycle

- Recognize the difference between data and information infrastructure and knowledge infrastructure

- Maintain the security and integrity of information

- Understand, develop, and conduct procedures for system backups

- Create a thorough training infrastructure that supports the BPO transition

Working with an outsourcing vendor involves the integration of a variety of formerly distinct systems, both technical and social. Previous chapters discussed the social aspects of project and relationship management, including the difficulties associated with intermingling organizational cultures and managing organizational change. This chapter focuses primarily on technical infrastructure issues that arise after the BPO project has been launched and operations have begun. These issues include hardware, software, knowledge, security, and training and support, some of which were addressed in the total cost management sections of Chapter 3.

The focus here is not on the *cost* elements of the infrastructure considerations, but on the *management* issues that will arise and questions that need to be asked and answered during the transition and operating phases of the BPO Life Cycle. Companies undertaking a BPO initiative may want to revisit their cost estimates as a result of the more detailed discussion of the technical issues contained in this chapter.

Fundamentally, the goal of infrastructure integration is to embed and reinforce the collaborative nature of the relationship between buyer and vendor. Before the interlinking of their respective systems, the two companies have interacted only on a surface level. There have been no process changes on either side and no threats to business continuity. The integration of buyer and vendor infrastructures represents a true turning point in the BPO relationship—the partners are now becoming familiar with one another. The transition phase is characterized by sharing systems, data, and knowledge. Each party now has additional risk exposure. The buyer is concerned about data and systems integrity. The vendor is concerned with meeting the contract terms established by the sales team. Cross-enterprise collaboration to improve performance must be the overriding objective for each organization.

There are a variety of infrastructures that must be managed during the transition and operating phases of the BPO Life Cycle. Though exceedingly interdependent, they can be divided into four sections:

1. Hardware infrastructure
2. Software infrastructure
3. Knowledge infrastructure
4. Training and support infrastructure

A truly effective BPO project will elevate itself beyond the service-level agreements (SLAs) established in the contract.[1] The project management plan discussed in Chapter 5 highlights the basic operating rules, and procedures for modifying them, that are freely agreed to by each side. Establishing a collaborative mindset that seeks to leverage economies of scale and each party's core business strengths can lead to amazing and unexpected results. However, if the BPO relationship is governed solely by the SLAs, the relationship will be more traditional, focusing on service delivery, monitoring, and meting out rewards and penalties. To achieve breakthrough results from the BPO project, the infrastructure needs to support that potential. This chapter addresses infrastructure issues from the perspective of creating the potential for breakthrough performance through cross-enterprise collaboration.[2]

Hardware Infrastructure

The first issue to consider with respect to the hardware infrastructure underlying the BPO project is whose systems to use. Because providing high levels of service in the specific business process is the vendor's core competence, their hardware capabilities usually outstrip those of the buyer. Despite this common circumstance, the decision to use the vendor's hardware system should not be based on technology maturity alone. Buyer and vendor must also consider other factors when determining whether to shift processes to the vendor's hardware.

Three Critical Considerations

Although there are many considerations that can affect this decision, three stand out:

1. Intent of the BPO agreement

2. Buyer's interest in developing and retaining new capacities

3. Location of the systems

Regarding the first point, firms that outsource primarily to save costs should leverage the vendor's systems, eliminating depreciating assets from the balance sheet and converting them to monthly pretax expenses. However, BPO buyers seeking to develop strategic advantages through the BPO project may elect to leverage and/or build their own hardware systems using the vendor's knowledge and experience. This ensures that the buyer will retain any competitive advantages realized through hardware advances if the contract with the vendor is terminated or not renewed.

The extent of the BPO buyer's interest in developing and retaining new capacities in the outsourced process is the second major determinant of whose hardware to use in the BPO project. Another consideration that affects this decision is the potential to develop synergies with other business units by building internal hardware maturity and capacity for the project. While scaling systems to meet the demands of the enhanced business process, the BPO buyer creates capacities that may be applicable to other units within the organization. These capacities are often unexpected and can improve performance across the organization. Relying on the vendor's hardware means forgoing development of internal capacities and the possibility of unexpected process improvements in other business units. Of course, this risk can be mitigated through a deep, collaborative buyer–vendor relationship that seeks to leverage hardware advances for process improvements no matter where the hardware resides or who has title to it.[3] The final consideration when assessing whose hardware to use is location. When a BPO buyer decides to use the vendor's hardware, that hardware is often located off the buyer's site. This is usually not a problem if the vendor is local or onshore in the United States. Problems may arise, however, when the vendor is offshore. As the BPO revolution continues, offshore locations may include increasingly remote regions of the world. BPO buyers must confirm the vendor's ability to obtain technical support and spare parts to maintain their systems and minimize downtime. Systems that are state-of-the-art but that have been damaged by an earthquake, political uprising, or other unexpected event are not much use if they cannot be repaired and placed back online in a hurry.

Infrastructure and Architecture

Regardless of whose hardware systems are used, the infrastructure compatibility between both organizations must be reviewed and managed. This is critical, because both organizations will rely on the combined system to provide transparency. One important distinction for BPO project managers to grasp is the difference between a system's infrastructure and its architecture:

- *Infrastructure.* Refers to the system's hardware components and their functionalities. The hardware infrastructure hosts a variety of applications that rely on the components of the infrastructure and management procedures (i.e., software distribution, backup, recovery, and capacity planning) to provide reliable, efficient services.
- *Architecture.* Refers to the configuration of the components— the way they are structured and the way they interact with one another.

177

TIPS & TECHNIQUES

Conducting an Infrastructure and Architecture Audit

When considering the hardware needed for a BPO project, the Project Management Team (PMT) must be aware of infrastructure and architecture issues. Because BPO projects require resource sharing regardless of where the bulk of the components reside, a complete audit of available resources and their configuration should be conducted. This will enable the PMT to:

- Avoid needless duplication of systems and services.
- Pinpoint gaps in infrastructure capability.
- Ensure infrastructure/business alignment.
- Ensure adequate scope of information technology (IT) components to accommodate service enhancements.
- Assess security issues associated with data and knowledge sharing over networks.
- Reengineer processes that are obviously inefficient or anachronistic.

In addition to this audit process, the BPO buyer should be prepared to pose six important questions to vendors:

❶ What operating system, Web server, commerce server, database management system, payment system, and proxy server does the vendor use?

❷ What are the security-level arrangements in terms of availability, performance, and security?

❸ How scalable is the BPO infrastructure? What are the scalable constraints?

❹ What is the aggregate bandwidth at the site locations?

❺ Is there any load-balancing scheme at the site?

❻ What type of redundancy is available at the site (i.e., server redundancy, uninterrupted power service; RAID [redundant array of independent disks], and multiple Internet backbone providers)?

Stated another way, an infrastructure model provides a description of hardware resources and their individual functions, whereas the architecture describes their interrelationships and the services that can be delivered. For example, a system's infrastructure may include e-mail servers and network cabling. Their arrangement into a specific architecture enables the delivery of e-mail services to specific groups of employees.

The system architecture designed for the BPO initiative will most often be based on the vendor's systems. At the same time, it is important to note that many BPO projects uncover inefficiencies in noncore processes and systems that are linked to the business process slated for outsourcing. The PMT should be trained to identify such inefficiencies as candidates for reengineering. Many outsourcing contracts allow for buyer–vendor cooperation to reengineer processes that are coupled to the outsourced process. Such cross-enterprise collaboration on reengineering buyer-side processes and systems is a vital component of transformational BPO.[4] Each reengineering initiative can be managed independently or as part of the PMT's charter. As the buyer systems interact with the more efficient vendor services, opportunities for reengineering will undoubtedly emerge. The PMT should stay vigilant for such opportunities, striving to ensure that buyer-side systems do not become the chief bottlenecks in constantly improving process flows.

Software Infrastructure

Software compatibility is often a difficult issue *within* an organization. Compatibility issues are amplified in a BPO relationship when attempting to bring buyer and vendor applications into alignment. Database issues will confront nearly every BPO relationship, as data sharing is the backbone of most BPO projects. While this discussion stops short of recommending how to get disparate databases to talk to one another, BPO project managers should be alert to the difficulties often encountered when two systems attempt to connect at the database level.

Organizations that use BPO to *improve* their service levels—as opposed to seeking mere cost savings—are those most likely to encounter difficulties because their internal systems may well lag behind the latest technology upgrades. The BPO vendor, however, has chosen to focus on the specific business process as its core business competence and is likely to be current in its software infrastructure, including its database systems. The greater the gap between buyer and vendor software maturity, the greater the challenges in database integration and data sharing. It is reasonable, if not expected, that the burden will be on the vendor to manage database integration. The cost, however, is likely to be borne, at least in part, by the buyer.

Publishing of Data and Information

In addition to the initial data integration challenges—which focus on getting the buyer and vendor systems to communicate with one another—another important challenge concerns data and information distribution and publishing. During the operating phase of the BPO Life Cycle, the vendor is performing service-related transactions that generate new business data and information. That information needs to be distributed to relevant databases and published to relevant screens for use by others in the buyer and vendor organizations. Thorough analysis of data flows is required to ensure, at a minimum, that the people who need the information generated by the outsourced transactions continue to receive it—and receive it in a familiar format and at the right time.[5]

In addition, the BPO buyer must be conscious of the potential hidden value in transaction information that is stored in a data warehouse and not destined for immediate additional processing. *Data mining* refers to the process of analyzing an organization's collected data that has not been immediately routed for additional processing. These data are stored in the data warehouse and often contain insights into customers and competitors that would otherwise have gone unnoticed.[6] The BPO buyer should ensure that the vendor captures and stores all transactional data that can later be mined for strategic insights.

Once the two systems have established database connectivity, their respective software applications must be able to communicate. This can pose a problem if there are a large number of applications, because many of them will not recognize one another. If the two software systems are unable to communicate, then an independent piece of software—called middleware—may be necessary.

Middleware: A Data Translator

Middleware is software that enables two noncompatible applications to communicate, acting as a data translator between the applications. If executable commands are needed, the logic scripts can be written and executed off the middleware platform, while delivering data to existing back-office databases via open database connectivity (ODBC) drivers. ODBC is a standard database access method developed by Microsoft. The goal of ODBC is to make it possible to access any data from any application, regardless of which database management system (DBMS) is handling the data. ODBC manages this by inserting a middle layer, called a database driver, between an application and the DBMS. The purpose of this layer is to translate the application's data queries into commands that the DBMS understands.

Admittedly, this is a cursory discussion of software compatibility. Suffice it to say, however, that a BPO buyer's technical support staff may point to the necessity of a middleware package to facilitate software integration with the vendor. This adds costs, of course, but the goal is to create as much interorganizational transparency as is required to perform services at the highest levels—and to support transactional data capture, storage, and mining.

Making the Buyer–Vendor Connection

In addition to the details of software and database compatibility, the BPO buyer must be concerned about the method that will be used to connect its systems with those of the vendor. Multiple alternatives exist:

- *Servers.* Buyers can use a single or multiple servers to connect with the vendor's system via a wide area network (WAN) or send the necessary information via electronic flat file.

- *Active server pages (ASPs).* Using ASPs on an application server allows the BPO partners to see and use familiar screens to conduct their jobs. The application servers typically use ODBC drivers to map into the back-office databases, enabling both companies to interact with real-time data.

- *Virtual private network (VPN).* In some cases, the BPO vendor's services may be so tightly integrated into the buyer's back office that the vendor requires full access to data systems. If that is the case, a common technique to facilitate full access is a global VPN. VPNs have become popular over the past several years, and third-party companies offer support service at reasonable prices.[7]

TIPS & TECHNIQUES

Licensing Agreement

A technology issue that will likely have to be managed in any BPO initiative is the licensing agreement that governs usage of the BPO buyer's software. Purchasing a software license, in most cases, does not legally authorize the buyer to use the software in every given networking scenario. For example, when a third party joins a network, the software company may require a client access license (CAL) for each additional party that accesses the system.

- *File transfers.* These have the greatest utility when the vendor is providing services that do not require access to the buyer's computer system. The file transfer method can be as simple as the vendor sending a weekly e-mail outlining all activity, sending a flat file, or setting up a basic electronic data interchange (EDI) translator.

Knowledge Infrastructure

Clearly, the data and information infrastructure is a vital part of any BPO relationship. Competitive businesses are data driven, and in many cases a large part of their overall value is derived from the industry and market data they have collected, stored, and analyzed. However, a company's knowledge infrastructure is even more important, because knowledge refers to the practical application of the analyzed data and information.

The knowledge infrastructure of the BPO buyer involves several components, some of which are directly affected by the BPO relationship. *Knowledge* is defined as "analyzed and applied information that helps the organization compete and grow." Data and information are generated by raw transactions; knowledge is generated by analysis and reflection on aggregated transactions.

Sources of Organizational Knowledge

Organizational knowledge comes from a variety of sources. One common source is analytic software that seeks patterns in transactional data and reports these patterns to human users as discussed in Chapter 1. For example, the balanced scorecard approach used by many companies today conveys aggregated and analyzed transactional information to the desktops of users who can apply that knowledge to their work. Sales managers who receive daily reports that aggregate real-time sales data will know when to crack the whip and when it is acceptable to relax a bit.

BPO buyers and vendors should ensure that the output provided by the buyer's analytic software systems before the BPO project is not corrupted or changed without intent. The systems used by the buyer before the BPO project may need to be upgraded or replaced, but such upgrades should not be made without a full understanding of who is using the generated knowledge and for how long. Knowledge output from an analytic software application may be distributed to multiple databases. If a new analytic package is introduced, each output database should be identified to ensure minimal disruption of internal workflows. Too often, a reengineering process in one business unit results in an unexpected loss of essential data in another. BPO project managers must always be mindful of the interdependence of data flows within an organization and between an organization and its various stakeholders. For example, many organizations routinely share data with suppliers and customers to create efficiencies and, in the case of customers, to increase perceived value and switching costs. The integrity of these data flows must be maintained.

Capturing Outsourced Knowledge

Outsourcing a business process means that the organization will not be exposed to the raw data that used to be transformed into knowledge by people within the organization. For example, as a result of outsourcing, the firm may no longer employ front-line workers who used to recognize data patterns and call attention to outliers, anomalies, and opportunities.

The outsourcing vendor can produce the knowledge previously generated by internal staff if appropriate incentives are established. Internal staff were motivated to recognize and discuss data patterns based on their commitment to the organization's strategic objectives, their interest in receiving greater compensation, and their desire to simplify their jobs. These incentives may not exist for the offshore agent, who may not

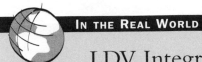

IN THE REAL WORLD

LDV Integrates Systems to Improve Performance

LDV started out as a division of British Leyland. When the U.K. manufacturing giant closed its doors, many industry observers believed that LDV, which builds commercial vehicles, would soon follow suit. But LDV was saved by a management buyout and today employs more than 1,000 people at its Birmingham factory.

LDV has broad expertise in the automotive market, but its niche also presents management with significant challenges. "We specialize in custom-designed vehicles, and rely heavily on our supply chain applications, which run on IBM mainframes," said Chris Linfoot, the company's IT director. "The problem is that those mainframes were designed to be used by Leyland, which had a far larger IT staff than we can afford."

For five years LDV had outsourced the maintenance of its mainframes to IBM, but Linfoot felt the company was not getting enough benefits from the arrangement. When the contract ended, he switched the outsourcing deal to Gedas, the information services arm of Volkswagen.

The outsourcing contract has allowed LDV to focus on what it does best—manufacturing vans and other commercial vehicles—while still benefiting from the mainframe applications.

LDV has already benefited from Gedas's expertise in automobile manufacturing. For example, Gedas has helped develop new processes that will eliminate the need for batch processing and enable the factory to operate 24 hours a day. "The result is that we are now on the verge of a major growth spurt which will see volume quadruple," said Linfoot. "*Outsourcing* one part of our business to a company which understands it so much better than a traditional service provider is a key part of that process."

Source: Adapted from Sally Whittle, "Who Can You Trust to Take Care of Business?" *Computer Weekly* (October 21, 2003): 48–49.

even be aware of nor deeply care about the industry or market of the BPO buyer.

To ensure that this valuable source of organizational knowledge is not lost in the operating phase of the BPO Life Cycle, the buyer and vendor should establish incentives for front-line agents (vendor employees) to seek and report data patterns that may result in process improvements. One way to address this issue is by specifying incentive terms in the BPO contract. However, the establishment of knowledge-generation incentives may be too granular for the BPO contract and may be better established in the project management plan. This provides greater flexibility to both parties to determine where the likely points of mission-critical knowledge generation are within the workflow and how to properly arrange incentives for individuals at those critical points.[8]

Maintaining Information Integrity and Security

Another consideration in the knowledge infrastructure of a BPO project is cross-enterprise knowledge management. In many cases, BPO buyers share mission-critical information with their vendor—information that is not only important for organizational processes but may also be of high interest to competitors. The criticality of this information creates two worries: maintaining information integrity and maintaining information security.

Maintaining information integrity means that the information shared between buyer and vendor organizations does not get corrupted or reconfigured. Data corruption would result in inappropriate conclusions and errant actions as a result of analysis of altered—and possibly false—data. Data reconfiguration refers to the potential that raw data has been altered in some way that makes it unreadable and unable to be converted into usable knowledge. Altered display screens are an example of data reconfiguration. Often, a BPO vendor uses proprietary data displays for internal use. These displays, if published to the BPO buyer as replace-

TIPS & TECHNIQUES

Security Questions for BPO Vendors

BPO buyers should thoroughly address a vendor's commitment and ability to maintain information security. This should include asking the questions such as:

- What is its security policy?
- What are its data backup and disaster-recovery procedures?
- How is the data safeguarded from that of its other customers?
- How is its data safeguarded from the vendor's own employees?
- How is the data insured with regard to security breaches?

ments for familiar screens, may render the data useless to the end user even though the integrity of the data has been carefully maintained. Displaying data in a new and unfamiliar user interface can befuddle—or at least frustrate—even the most adaptable users.

When entering into an outsourcing partnership, the buyer and vendor, in effect, become one. For the BPO initiative to produce results that meet and exceed expectations, there must be transparency between both entities. However, when two computer systems located in separate locations begin interfacing, *maintaining information security* becomes a major issue. BPO buyers must ensure that the vendor will adhere to the buyer's security policies and that all work done adheres to up-to-date security procedures.

Assuring Internet Security

In many cases, the BPO buyer and vendor communicate with one another via the Internet. When entering into a new BPO relationship, both organizations should review their Internet security policies. When developing an Internet security policy, BPO buyers should keep the following points in mind:

- *Limit access.* Many security breaches come from within an organization; thus, the fewer people with access to the inner workings of the system, the better.

- *Establish granting privileges.* A rigorous procedure should be in place for granting and revoking rights of access, and granting privileges should be recorded and made available to both client and BPO partner.

- *Streamline hardware and software between the two organizations.* Complex systems are more open to attack.

- *Develop a secure password policy.* This should include not allowing users to choose simple or obvious passwords.

- *Have backup and emergency procedures in place before going live.* This should include data backup, disaster recovery, responding to security breaches, and identifying those actions to be taken in the event of a breach.

- *Implement an external audit.* Security policies should be audited by an external professional organization, which should also be on call if a major breach occurs.

Training and Support Infrastructure

Most of the problems employees will experience during a project will be unrelated to the hardware or software infrastructure associated with BPO. They will be more likely related to failures in understanding new workflows, work procedures, and work responsibilities. From the apocryphal user who cannot find the "Any" key ("Press any key to continue") to the individual struggling to find data that, without warning, now appears under a new field name, there are always problems with human adaptation to new systems. When the buyer and vendor system architectures come together in a BPO project, there will be workflow and responsibility changes. To avoid some of the problems that arise from process-related changes, and to ensure a smooth transition to the new system, training should be provided to everyone—even those who are adamant that they do not need to be trained.

One hurdle that faces many BPO project managers with respect to training employees and getting them to be more self-sufficient is obtaining support from midlevel managers. This is primarily because the middle manager is trying to learn the new processes while maintaining the unit's productivity. This juggling act can be challenging in the throes of a major BPO-based business transformation.

Perhaps the most compelling argument in favor of a thorough training infrastructure to support the BPO transition is that employee training has been shown to be an important differentiator between BPO projects that succeed and those that fail.[9] When training is neglected, the chance that buyer-side employees will be surprised and/or disappointed with new procedures and workflows increases. BPO project managers will have a small window of opportunity during the transition phase to win converts to the new routines and work patterns.

In Chapter 5, we referred to two different types of obstructionists who may block or sabotage the BPO project. Some of these people can be won over via a vigorous training and support regimen. Asking people to participate and take on a leadership role in some aspect of the BPO transition is an excellent way to counter their obstruction. For example, delegating responsibility for training others on the new procedures, along with appropriate levels of accountability for the success of the transition, is an effective project management tactic. It is nearly impossible for someone to be involved in training others without developing enthusiasm for and interest in the training topic. Public performance, even if not necessarily freely chosen, leads to a phenomenon known as *social facilitation*.[10] People—including those with a tendency toward obstructionism—simply perform at a higher level when they are in a social setting.

BPO project managers can co-opt potential obstructers by getting them involved in the training and support offered to employees in the BPO transition phase.

The content of employee training offered during the BPO transition should include a detailed and thorough review of new work procedures, responsibilities, and expectations. In developing a BPO-related training and support regimen, organizations should also consider:

- Developing a clear set of standard operating procedures (SOPs)
- Training programs that revolve around the SOPs
- Conducting multiple training sessions:
  - Train in a group setting.
  - Train while working alongside employees during their workday.
  - When answering questions, always refer back to the SOP.
  - Final training should be completed after 60 days (refresher).
- Not taking training lightly

Modular Design for Training

Design of the training should be modular, with each module independently constructed and each focusing on a specific aspect of the new SOPs. Modularization of the training allows managers and employees to determine who needs to attend which modules and enables greater training depth in each module. If training is not modularized, it often is either too detailed for some users who already understand a process or not detailed enough for those who are unfamiliar with or new to the process. Modularization allows training designers to deliver both depth and scope, while ensuring that employees have opportunities to select the training sessions (or for managers to appoint them to training sessions) from which they can truly benefit. No one enjoys sitting through a training session that relays information he or she already knows and understands. Carefully developed two- to four-hour training modules help avoid training overkill, while providing adequate coverage of the knowledge gaps.

Training Vendor-Side Employees

A common error that hampers BPO projects is a failure to train vendor-side employees, probably because of the erroneous assumption that the vendor is expert in the business process and therefore does not need training. This is true in some cases—especially those that involve an onshore outsourcing relationship—but it is prudent to review training needs of the BPO vendor.[11] Some types of vendor-side training that are being provided to accelerate the transition to the BPO operating phase include:

- Cultural adaptation training to help buyer and vendor employees adapt to one another
- Language training, including voice and accent modification training, to reduce communication barriers
- Training on laws and customs of the BPO buyer
- Training on culture and lifestyles of the BPO buyer's customers[12]
- Training on differing management and leadership styles of the BPO buyer

Training should also be designed to integrate the cultures of the BPO buyer and vendor. This may include some training offered at each location to enable key employees to experience the culture and work habits of their BPO partner firm. In some cases, BPO buyer and vendor employees work side by side for a period of time in a form of on-the-job training that facilitates cross-enterprise understanding.[13]

Establishing a Systematic Support System

Merging two diverse organizations and their various infrastructures is daunting. The BPO transition phase is the most difficult of the life cycle and the one where future operating patterns, routines, and procedures are established and frozen into place. In the best of all possible worlds, the procedures established lead to a highly efficient interorganizational system that runs trouble-free for years. Of course, this is not the best of all possible worlds, and problems arise in even the most carefully crafted systems. To deal with ongoing challenges to system integrity caused by breakdowns or other factors, a systematic support system, troubleshooting approach, and record-keeping strategy should be established.

The support system established for the BPO transition and operating phases must be adequate to meet the needs of the buyer and vendor organizations alike. Each will face unique challenges based on exposure to new operating procedures, in addition to the challenges associated with the merging of two independent work cultures. The support system established to manage the technical issues that arise should be modeled on the common help desk approach used by many IT departments. The only consideration unique to a BPO project is which firm will manage the help desk function. The vendor should inherit most of the responsibility for troubleshooting and supporting the outsourced process. This should be part of the contract and should have its own SLAs. However, because the BPO vendor is usually geographically distant from the buyer—maybe overseas—the buyer should have on-site support personnel who may be on the vendor payroll but accountable to a buyer-side manager.

Summary

The process of integrating BPO buyer and vendor infrastructures is the beginning of the operating phase of the BPO project. The goal of this integration is to embed and reinforce the collaborative nature of the buyer–vendor relationship. While there is an array of infrastructures that must be managed during the transition and operating phases of the BPO Life Cycle, they can generally be broken into four categories: (1) hardware, (2) software, (3) knowledge, and (4) training and support. As the process continues, key issues with arise. These include whether to use the vendor's or the buyer's system; how to manage the challenges of data exchange; assuring that analytic software systems are not corrupted or changed without intent; implementing effective system backup and security guidelines; and developing training programs that counter employee obstruction, are modular in design, and recognize the need for training vendor-side employees.

Endnotes

1. Jane C. Linder, "Transformational Outsourcing," *MIT Sloan Management Review* (Winter 2004): 52–58.

2. The term *cross-enterprise collaboration* is normally used in supply-chain management literature. However, its definition of transparency between organizations with the goal of creating strategic advantages for both firms is pertinent to the BPO relationship. See Donald J. Bowersox, David J. Closs, and Theodore P. Stank, "How to Master Cross-Enterprise Collaboration," *Supply Chain Management Review* (July/August 2003): 18–26.

3. John Storck and Patricia A. Hill, "Knowledge Diffusion Through 'Strategic Communities,'" *MIT Sloan Management Review* (Winter 2000): 63–74.

4. "Transformational Outsourcing—It's All in the Contract," *Global Computing Services* (July 25, 2003): 4.

5. "Outsourcing: A Global Success Story," *Logistics Management* (February 2003): 60–62.

6. Shoshanna Zuboff, *In the Age of the Smart Machine: The Future of Work and Power* (New York: Basic Books, 1988).

7. Norbert Turek, "New VPNs for a Global Economy," *InformationWeek* (August 20, 2000): 57–62.

8. Daniela Grigori, Fabio Casati, Malu Castellanos, Umesh Dayal, Ming-Chien Shan, Mehmet Sayal, "Business Process Intelligence," *Computers in Industry* (April 2004): 321–343.

9. "Shared Services: The Benefits & Challenges," *Global Computing Services* (July 25, 2003): 4–6.

10. Judith Platania and Gary P. Moran, "Social Facilitation as a Function of the Mere Presence of Others," *Journal of Social Psychology* (April 2001): 190–197.

11. Martyn Hart, "Call Center Offshoring May Damage Firms," *People Management* (December 4, 2003): 7.

12. Linda Punch, "The Global Back Office: Beyond the Hype," *Credit Card Management* (January 2004): 26–32.

13. William W. Lewis, "Educating Global Workers," *McKinsey Quarterly* (2003 Special Edition): 4–5.

CHAPTER 7

Business Risks and Mitigation Strategies

After reading this chapter, you will be able to:

- Identify, manage, and mitigate potential BPO-related business risks

- Recognize the seven primary areas of risk that exist

- Assess risks regarding equal employment, labor laws, immigration, and foreign trade agreements

- Scrutinize the human resource (HR) practices of potential vendors, and avoid risks related to vendors whose business practices may be unacceptable in the United States

- Assess the organization's ability to undertake a BPO initiative and thus reduce project risks

- Manage expectations of the BPO project at multiple levels

- Recognize the value of setting and complying with best-practice standards—including the use of third parties—to mitigate intellectual property (IP) risks

- Minimize or avoid legal issues to facilitate more favorable contracts

- Anticipate potential problems and issues within a vendor organization

- Overcome the challenges to extracting maximum value from the BPO initiative

- Estimate and plan for the potential of unusual or unexpected events that can affect the BPO plan

Because it is the catalyst of such significant changes for the organization, a BPO initiative is also associated with business risks. The pioneering firms that led the current wave of interest in outsourcing were Global 2000–sized companies with the capacity to absorb occasional business mistakes, even relatively large ones. When IBM outsources a sizable portion of its programming to India, it is a risk, but not as big a risk as when a small enterprise stakes the future of its business on the programming abilities of a little-known group of Bangalore-based programmers. As the size of the outsourcing projects increases in proportion to the size of the BPO buyer, business risk also increases proportionately. In order for BPO to become a source of competitive advantage for small to medium-sized enterprises (SMEs), proven techniques for managing and mitigating risks must be developed.

Fortunately, the BPO pioneers have not only reaped tremendous advantages from BPO, but they have also progressed along the learning curve, suffering many painful lessons along the way. It is doubtful that every BPO horror story has been written. However, many have been, and the lessons learned can help the next generation of BPO buyers avoid writing the sequel.

This chapter explores the most common BPO risk factors and discusses effective management techniques for mitigating those risks. These factors will be examined from the perspective of SMEs that seek to gain their fair share of the advantages offered by BPO. Lacking the capital and other resources to absorb the impact of major strategic decision errors, SME executives and managers must be vigilant about risk avoidance and mitigation. The discussion focuses on seven primary areas, each of which should be addressed in a thorough risk-management strategy developed by the Project Management Team (PMT):

1. Human capital risks
2. Project risks

3. IP risks

4. Legal risks

5. Vendor organizational risks

6. Value risks

7. Force majeure risks

From the outset, this book has emphasized that BPO is a sociotechnical phenomenon. The convergence of the six major BPO drivers was not anticipated or planned by any government or international agency. Managers and executives employed in organizations seeking to outsource business processes cannot rely on their business school education or their experience to help them deal with BPO opportunities and challenges. Not many have led business transformation opportunities that comprise the many facets of BPO—technical *and* social.

The following discussion partially fills that educational and experiential gap, but there is more to be learned about each risk area than is covered here. BPO managers should actively seek to engage in continuing education and learning about BPO even during the execution of a real-time project. As BPO is evolving rapidly, the pursuit of new knowledge beyond this book will be critical to the success of both ongoing and future BPO initiatives.

Human Capital Risks

Chapter 6 examined the challenges associated with managing the organizational changes that go hand in hand with a BPO project. Change management is an HR issue, involving a well-understood pattern of overcoming resistance, instituting changes, and reestablishing standard operating procedures (SOPs). Some change management consultants have expressed this as unfreezing–moving–refreezing the organization.[1]

This section does not address the risks related to change management; rather, it focuses on the technical risks involved with the thorny

How *Not* to Manage an RIF

As a 48-year-old senior engineer at WatchMark Corp., a Bellevue, Washington, software company, Myra Bronstein had spent three years searching for bugs in the company's software. She knew things were not going well; she had been asked to log 12- to 18-hour shifts frequently, her boss reiterating that the company's success depended on her "hard work and efforts." So when she received an e-mail in March 2003 instructing her to come to a meeting in the boardroom the next day, she began to worry.

Bronstein logged on to a Yahoo users' group for WatchMark employees. There, in a post written by "Saddam Hussein," was an ominous note stating: "For all the quality assurance engineers reading this, your jobs are gone." At that very moment, it said, their replacements were on their way from India.

The next morning, a Friday, Bronstein and some 60 others were told they were being terminated. Some left immediately; others, like Bronstein, were asked to stay on for several weeks to train the new employees. "Our severance and unemployment were contingent on training the replacements," she said. And so the next week, Bronstein walked into a room to find her old coworkers on one side and the new group from India on the other. "It was like a sock hop where everyone is lined up against the wall blinking at each other," she said. In an attempt to lighten the mood, her boss said she would like to introduce the old staff to the new staff, while the VP of engineering chimed in with familiar words. "We're depending on you to help this company succeed," he said.

Sources: Jennifer Reingold et al., "Into Thin Air," *FastCompany* (April 2004): 76–82; and John Cook, "Debate Over Outsourcing Heats Up, Ignited by Election-Year Politics," *Seattle Post-Intelligencer* (February 12, 2004).

issues of equal employment opportunity, immigration, and foreign trade regulations. Each of these topics touches the BPO project on the margins and must be understood and managed.

Onshore outsourcing usually has minimal human capital risks because it is strongly in the domestic BPO *vendor's* interest to understand and comply with all U.S. employment laws and regulations. Furthermore, the vendor is highly motivated to assist clients with any labor issues they may face as a result of engaging vendors in an outsourcing relationship. The human capital issues most likely to arise in an onshore outsourcing project are those associated with equal employment opportunity regulations. For example, BPO buyers must be especially careful when outsourcing results in reductions in force (RIFs). Such reductions must be handled in a manner that is transparently related to business interests and has not selectively targeted a protected class of individuals. This risk can be managed by establishing formal RIF policies and procedures as outlined in Chapter 5.

Labor-Related Risks

Other human capital risks associated with onshore outsourcing concern those that stem from collective bargaining and labor relations laws and regulations. For example, the U.S. Supreme Court has established basic guidelines governing whether and when subcontracting should be deemed a mandatory subject of bargaining under the National Labor Relations Act (NLRA). Beginning in the early 1980s, the National Labor Relations Board (NLRB) issued several decisions that created additional uncertainty when evaluating the bargaining status of *outsourcing* or subcontracting decisions. The NLRB's lack of clarity on the obligations of employers in collective bargaining is unlikely to be resolved anytime soon. To reduce risk, companies should consult with labor attorneys as part of the BPO opportunity analysis to determine the likely disposition of their preferred strategy and its implications for possible liability exposure.[2]

Understanding Labor Laws in Non-U.S. Countries

BPO buyers that use an offshore outsourcing vendor can benefit from an absence of many of the employment liabilities present in the United States. Many foreign countries do not have laws governing matters such as workplace discrimination, sexual harassment, or privacy. At the same time, companies must understand the labor laws that govern their outsourcing vendor. India, for example, has a radically different system of employment law than the United States. "At will" employment, which allows U.S. employers to easily terminate or lay off employees, does not exist there. Under a much more restrictive concept called *termination indemnity*," employers must follow a lengthy notification process before letting Indian employees go. They must also indemnify employees for some of the wages they would have earned if they had remained on the job. Failure to follow the appropriate process can result in fines for an employer operating in India. Additionally, employers cannot enter into contracts under which individual workers sign away such rights. Similar employment laws restricting an employer's right to terminate workers exist in many countries that are hotbeds of outsourcing.

The more restrictive labor laws in foreign countries can limit the flexibility BPO buyers seek. For example, a BPO Project Management Team may recognize the need to reorganize a vendor's process to improve it. In some countries, it can be difficult for a company to restructure or change its operating strategies. Even moving an employee to a new work site could be a challenge in the foreign vendor's regulatory environment. The ability to restructure the organization—which is taken for granted in the United States—can be more difficult and riskier in many foreign countries.[3]

Study Vendor Labor Practices

The most important risk mitigation strategy regarding human capital is to vigorously scrutinize vendor labor practices during the selection phase. The BPO buyer can avoid future headaches by seeking vendors whose HR practices and policies resemble their own. Beyond that, it is also important to assess the professionalism of the vendor in its HR procedures and policies.

TIPS & TECHNIQUES

Identifying HR Professionalism in Vendors

Although difficult to define with precision, a vendor's labor practices can be earmarked. In general, a higher level of HR professionalism is characterized by:

- Turnover ratios that exceed local averages and approach the rates of U.S. professional firms
- A clean work environment that includes professional markers such as individual work areas, private conference facilities, a reception area, security, and employees wearing business attire
- Employee policy handbooks, and employees who understand their rights and responsibilities
- A current organizational chart with most positions filled
- Employee grievance procedures with evidence that grievances have been raised and effectively addressed (Be wary of vendors that claim they have never had a grievance.)

Sweatshop Risk

HR risks associated with offshore outsourcing also include the potential implications of practices acceptable in the foreign jurisdiction but unacceptable to consumers in the United States. The most common example of this is the so-called sweatshop labor practices that have damaged the image of firms such as Nike and Wal-Mart. Working with foreign companies whose HR practices are patently offensive to U.S. consumer sensitivities poses the risk of potential backlash if those practices are exposed. The BPO buyer, although not directly responsible for the offensive practices, is nonetheless considered to be an enabler because it has a contract with the vendor. To mitigate this risk, it is imperative that BPO buyers regularly assess the HR practices of the vendor. Better still, the buyer can protect itself by specifying minimally acceptable labor standards in the BPO contract. The contract should also spell out metrics that will enable the buyer to hold the vendor accountable to those standards.

Another human capital risk centers on potential legislation in the United States to limit foreign workers' ability to service U.S. clients on guest worker visas. In addition, bills to ban the outsourcing of government service contracts to foreign vendors have surfaced at the state level. These measures pose risks to organizations seeking to use offshore vendors because costs are involved in reabsorbing processes that had been outsourced.

Project Risks

Project risks are defined as those that have the potential to prevent the BPO initiative from not providing the cost savings, strategic advantages, or productivity improvements anticipated. The reasons for these risks are too numerous to list. Unexpected incompatibilities between software infrastructures could prove intractable and lead to delays, cost overruns, and lost business. The cultures of the two companies may pose unyielding challenges that become more trouble than they are worth. Changes in U.S. or foreign labor laws could upend the cost equations that had been the primary reason for the offshore outsourcing.

Mitigating Project Risks

To mitigate project risks, the BPO buyer should first assess its readiness to undertake the outsourcing project before making the leap. This includes an analysis of three key factors:

1. *Organization's ability to adapt to change.* Organizations with a poor track record in managing large-scale change are at a higher risk of project failure than those with a record of successful change management. An organization's record of success in this area reflects its culture and is likely to be consistent in the BPO initiative.

2. *Presence of an internal BPO champion.* An internal champion, especially one with broad influence within the organization, can reduce project risk. This person can be relied on to work long hours and lay awake nights thinking about solutions to project problems when other members of the PMT are sleeping well.

TIPS & TECHNIQUES

Value Horizon

One way to mitigate risks associated with project timing is to develop a reasonable value horizon. The term *value horizon* refers to the amount of value the organization expects to receive from the BPO project in a specific amount of time. For example, an organization that expects to reduce costs by 25 percent within three months may not be able to realize that value horizon because of project implementation costs. However, a 25 percent cost savings within two years may be achievable and would set the appropriate value expectations.

3. *Time available to make the transition and ramp up to full operational mode.* In general, the less time available for the transition, the higher the risk. It is often not practical to move all of a process to an offshore BPO vendor at once. Buyers should increase the time available to implement a BPO transition, building on successes along the way.

Risk of Unrealistic Expectations

The PMT often ignores the risks associated with unrealistic expectations on the part of the BPO buyer's executive team. Expectations can be managed at four levels:[4]

1. *Upward expectations management.* Refers to the procedures the PMT follows to ensure that the organization's executive team (and the BPO project Steering Team) is informed about project risks, potential costs, and mitigation strategies.

2. *Downward expectations management.* Refers to the challenge of managing employee expectations as the project unfolds.

3. *Horizontal expectations management.* Refers to handling expectations of managers in nonoutsourced functions.

4. *External expectations management.* Refers to the process of dealing with expectations of customers, suppliers, and other stakeholders outside the organization who have a need to know.

Upward Expectations Management

Managing senior leadership expectations is critical to the BPO project. Too-high expectations among senior managers can lead to overly critical feedback and potential plug pulling on a project that cannot meet excessively lofty expectations.[5] With the current level of media attention and hype that surrounds outsourcing, elevated and even unreasonable expectations among senior management should be expected. The PMT must ensure that senior managers are aware of the challenges an offshore BPO project faces and manage expectations accordingly.[6] Some have called this process *managing up.*[7] There are many effective techniques for managing up. Of course, this can be a delicate process because managing expectations up the chain of command may also often require that senior leaders be educated on technical or other issues.[8] To manage the expectations of senior leaders, the PMT should develop a project plan that articulates not only the problems and challenges likely to be encountered, but also those that have a lower probability of occurring. A good technique for communicating risk and managing expectations is to develop a BPO risk-probability matrix (Exhibit 7.1). The matrix will

---

EXHIBIT 7.1

Sample BPO Risk-Probability Matrix

Risk	Probability	Cost	Mitigation Tactics
Implementation will take longer than expected	95%	10%	Bonus plan, penalties
One or more key staff will resign	60–70%	2%	Retention program, training
Hardware/software inadequate for project	30–40%	5–8%	Vendor agreement to absorb costs
Customers will be dissatisfied or lost	10–15%	5%	Customer training, monitoring
Legal issues in foreign country	2–5%	10–15%	Top U.S. legal team support
Mission-critical data will be lost or damaged	1%	NA	QC program, mirror backup
War breaks out in vendor country	<1%	50%	Mirror backup in U.S.

---

include as many *reasonable* risks as the PMT can envision, including those that are classifiable as worst-case risks. The matrix will also include the mitigation tactics that are either in place or that will be mobilized in the event that the risk becomes real.

The BPO risk-probability matrix should be widely circulated and updated as needed. This document will serve as the starting point for understanding the wide range of potential risks associated with the project and their potential costs. In Exhibit 7.1, costs are expressed as a percentage of total project costs. It is important to note that the cost figures expressed in the BPO risk-probability matrix are *in addition to* those already agreed to in the BPO contract; in other words, they are meant to specify potential cost overruns.

Another effective technique for managing the expectations of the executive team is to include one or more senior leaders on the PMT. This individual will serve in a liaison role and maintain communications between the PMT and the executive team. The liaison will be *responsible* for regularly communicating BPO project results to the executive team and for feedback to the PMT. Importantly, the senior leader assigned to the liaison role on the PMT will be *accountable* to both the PMT and the executive team. This dual accountability should make the senior leader a true member of the PMT, ensure that the role is taken seriously, and add value to the expectations management task.

Horizontal Expectations Management

Managing horizontally means ensuring that managers of functions not being outsourced are informed and aware of potential risks. All BPO projects have potential cross-functional impact on organizational processes and workflow. Regardless of the process outsourced, it is likely that the output of that process is utilized by others within the organization. Changes to that output—whether in quality, quantity, or timing—

can affect the ability of internal functional units to maintain their SOPs. Managing expectations horizontally means minimizing workflow surprises and bringing managers from the nonoutsourced functions into the workflow redesign process. It would be disastrous to simply launch a BPO project without first determining in detail the effects of process output changes on units that depend on that output. Managers who are surprised by changes in data quality, quantity, or timing will defend the integrity of their work units and may become obstructionists to the BPO project.

External Expectations Management

Customers, suppliers, and others external to the organization may also have a vested interest in the BPO project. Customer reactions to BPO have been precipitated by several different factors. Some customers are concerned about BPO from a political perspective—they are worried about outsourcing jobs to offshore workers, for example. Dell responded to such political pressures when it pulled some of its technical support work in-house after outsourcing most of it to India.[9] Organizations need to consider BPO as a political issue that may affect customer perceptions. Communications with customers who are concerned about outsourcing jobs may include a recitation of the benefits they are likely to receive as a result of the outsourcing project. It may also include a statement about the domestic jobs the company has created and the number of new opportunities that may be generated as a result of moving some lower value-adding jobs to foreign labor markets.

The PMT should manage suppliers in much the same way it manages the expectations of internal managers whose functions are linked via workflow to the outsourced process. Suppliers linked to the outsourced process should also be included in workflow redesign so they are aware of changes and know whom to contact in case of disruptions or inefficiencies.

Managing expectations is not difficult, but this process is often over-looked because it involves proactive decision making and confronting problems before they arise. Engaging everyone—internally and externally—whose responsibilities, livelihood, or performance capabilities may be affected by the BPO project is the goal of the PMT. The PMT must communicate with these individuals (and groups, in some cases) to manage their expectations and to increase the amount of slack available in the event that some things go wrong (and they almost always will). If the goodwill of these stakeholders is won early in the process, and expectations are appropriately managed along the way, the PMT will have more latitude and time to fix problems that arise. Failure to properly manage expectations means that some will be out to kill the project at the first signs of trouble.

Intellectual Property Risks

Most businesses have a significant amount of sensitive information, including trade secrets, business plans, and proprietary business knowledge. Safeguarding critical business information is a concern, even in the United States. Threats to information security, including theft by company insiders, former employees, and computer hackers, abound. Offshore outsourcing presents different—and in some cases, more potent—threats than the domestic variety. Legal standards and business practices governing whether and how sensitive information should be guarded vary around the world.

Industry-Specific Guidelines

Some industry groups, such as banks and financial services firms, have developed stringent guidelines for organizations to follow to secure their proprietary information. The Bank Industry Technology Secretariat (BITS), for example, released security guidelines as an addendum to an existing framework for managing business relationships with IT service providers. The BITS goal is to help financial services firms streamline the outsourcing evaluation process and better manage the risks of handing over control of key corporate systems to vendors.[10] The BITS IT Service Providers Working Group developed the BITS Framework for Managing Technology Risk for IT Service Provider Relationships (Framework) in 2001. Although the original Framework provides an industry approach to outsourcing, additional regulatory and industry pressures and issues have emerged.

To address these changes, the Working Group updated the Framework with further considerations for disaster recovery, security audits and assessments, vendor management, and cross-border considerations. The Framework is intended to be used as part of, and in supplement to, the financial services company's due diligence process associated with defining, assessing, establishing, supporting, and managing a business relationship for outsourced IT services.

The U.S. Federal Trade Commission (FTC) has developed so-called Safeguard Rules to govern the security of customer information used and managed by domestic firms. These rules implement the provisions of the Gramm–Leach–Bliley Act, which requires the FTC to establish standards of information security for financial institutions. Penalties for failure to comply with FTC rules are up to $11,000 per violation (which may be assessed daily) and exposure to lawsuits claiming any harm to customers as a result of noncompliance.[11]

HIPAA Raises Concerns in Health Care

The Health Insurance Portability and Accountability Act of 1996 (HIPAA) has led to a host of security risk management concerns for health care institutions that outsource processes requiring electronic transmission of patient information. HIPAA is designed to protect confidential health care information through improved security standards and federal privacy legislation. It defines requirements for storing patient information before, during, and after electronic transmission. It also identifies compliance guidelines for critical business tasks such as risk analysis, awareness training, audit trail, disaster recovery plans, and information access control and encryption. There are 18 information security standards in three areas that must be met to ensure compliance with the HIPAA Security Rule. These areas are:

1. *Administrative safeguards.* Documented policies and procedures for day-to-day operations; managing the conduct of employees with electronic protected health information (EPHI); and managing the selection, development, and use of security controls

2. *Physical safeguards.* Security measures meant to protect an organization's electronic information systems, as well as related buildings and equipment, from natural hazards, environmental hazards, and unauthorized intrusion

3. *Technical safeguards.* Security measures that specify how to use technology to protect EPHI, particularly controlling access to it

Best Practices and Standards

The most effective information security risk management strategy is to adopt and comply with best practices and standards. Tort law in the United States includes four possible means by which a firm may be found liable for information security lapses: (1) duty, (2) negligence, (3) damage, and (4) cause. Duty refers to whether the organization has a responsibility to safeguard information. That duty is not in doubt in today's security-conscious environment. Negligence refers to an outright breach of the duty to safeguard information. It asks: "Is there evidence that the organization did not fulfill its duty of care?" Damage refers to whether there is harm to someone (the plaintiff) as a result of negligence. Cause refers to the question of whether the negligence led to or was the primary cause of the damage.

To manage the information security risk, BPO vendor organizations should adopt and be able to prove compliance with global best practices and standards. Many firms turn to managed-security providers (MSPs) to assist them in managing this risk. Good MSPs provide valuable analysis and reporting of threat events, supplementing the efforts of in-house security personnel. They do this by sifting through vast amounts of data in order to uncover, identify, and prioritize security vulnerabilities that must be addressed.[12] The best MSPs provide BPO buyers with:

- The ability to compare and correlate multiple monitoring points and to distinguish between false positives and actual threats

- Skilled experts on duty around the clock to assess and react to each threat in real time

- The ability to combine existing technology with expert analysis to look for anomalous behavior

- The ability to develop custom monitoring for specific networks or systems, including the development of an "attack signature" for each new vulnerability threat.

Using a third party to manage information security helps relieve the organization of information security concerns, but it does not remove liability if there is a security breach.[13] Liability cannot be transferred to a third party, unless the buyer invests in appropriate insurance policies. Exhibit 7.2 provides separate lists of responsibilities for MSPs and clients in maintaining information security.[14]

A good source of security risk management guidelines, policies, and best practices is the SANS Institute Web site (*www.sans.org*). The SANS (SysAdmin, Audit, Network, Security) Institute was established in 1989 as a cooperative research and education organization.

EXHIBIT 7.2

Outsourcer and Client Information Security Responsibilities

MSP	Client
Installs and maintains data security software.	Defines business needs and identifies data security issues.
Writes and maintains data center data security policies and procedures.	Writes and maintains internal data security policies and procedures.
Quality ensures client's logon ID structure and access rules.	Defines structure for logon IDs and access rules.
Establishes logon IDs and access rules according to agreed-on specifications.	Approves logon IDs and access rules as implemented.
Provides data for violation reports.	Updates logon IDs.
Supports client liaison to internal users and customers as needed.	Investigates and resolves violation reports.
Supports client training through technology transfer; may deliver training on contract basis.	Acts as liaison between outsourcer and internal users and customers.
Upholds service level agreements and enforces policies and procedures to protect all clients.	
Implements regulatory compliance procedures in a timely fashion.	

Legal Risks

Legal risks associated with offshore outsourcing are legion, and their threat is made worse by the relative lack of legal precedent. For example, there currently are no clear legal rules governing the extent to which remedies can be extracted from a BPO vendor in the case of a security breach or other gross malfeasance. Countries differ in their laws for foreign firms seeking damages from private enterprises.

Chapter 4 discussed details of the BPO contract and the legal relationship between BPO buyer and vendor. This governing document provides a framework for the buyer–vendor relationship. Today, many law firms and consultancies specialize in assisting BPO buyers in developing contract terms that are favorable and enforceable. Of course, each contract must foster and promote the BPO relationship. In an offshore BPO project, the BPO buyer may have to concede some governing jurisdiction to the vendor's home country. That is, it may not be possible to draft contracts with offshore vendors that demand all legal conflicts be decided in the buyer's preferred jurisdiction. Some give and take may be required on different contract elements, with some potential areas of conflict to be decided in a domestic forum, some in a forum preferred by the vendor, and others in an international forum such as the International Arbitration Association. BPO buyers should mix and match forums to ensure that matters of potentially greatest impact to competitive ability are decided in their preferred forum. This can be achieved if there is a willingness to concede that matters of less importance can be decided elsewhere.

One technique that has been effective for avoiding legal disputes is to split outsourcing contracts depending on different deliverables and service-level agreements (SLAs). For example, many firms outsource software development as well as IT management to third-party vendors. A BPO buyer would be wise to split the software development contract from the IT services contract. IT management services are generally governed by SLAs that require regular fee payments. However, software development fees should be payable at development milestones—with a substantial portion of the fee withheld until acceptance of the final code.[15] Splitting the contract so that standard service provisions are kept distinct from software development reduces the risk of financing the development of code that does not perform as expected.

Firms should also be careful to separate continuous service or trans-action-related terms from those that concern development of some type of output, such as software or knowledge that is the property of the BPO buyer. The transaction-related services are usually covered in the SLAs and are paid on a regular basis. Development contracts should be treated separately. It is reasonable for the BPO buyer to withhold a substantial portion of the development contract fees until the final product has been delivered and tested.

Vendor Organizational Risks

The risks associated with the BPO vendor's organization are perhaps the most difficult to accept because they are not easy to control. This risk is also enhanced when the vendor is offshore. The risks associated with the vendor organization can range from business practices to authenticity of certification and reference claims.

Vendor business practices can vary greatly around the world. Practices that are clearly prohibited or considered highly questionable in the United States can be routine in the vendor's home country. The problems of bribes, kickbacks, or money exchanged under the table have affected U.S. businesses abroad in a wide range of industries. The U.S. Foreign Corrupt Practices Act of 1977 is designed to discourage domestic companies from participating in practices abroad that are proscribed at home. Most BPO vendor companies were founded after the 1977 act was passed and are generally managed by individuals who are sensitive to the need to conform to its strictures. Market-based governance mechanisms also compel vendors to conform to U.S. standards. Still, the potential for abuse is present, and the frequency of abuse may increase in the Wild West atmosphere that is shaping up overseas as more and more vendors seek to strike it rich in BPO gold.

Another risk concerns the potential for vendors to overstate their competencies and to exaggerate the business and technical certifications they possess and the clients they serve. This risk can be mitigated through comprehensive due diligence that insists on objective proof of certifications and permission to talk to representatives from the vendor's client list. Vendors that refuse to share certification evidence or balk at client referrals should be treated with caution.

Vendor organizational risk also includes its HR practices. Many manufacturers that chose to outsource to foreign companies turned a blind eye to labor practices long banned in the United States. Child labor, excessively long hours, and outright sexual and other forms of harassment or discrimination are not uncommon in some foreign labor markets. Firms choosing to outsource business processes should consider the labor practices of the vendor and determine whether the risk of participating in domestically reviled practices abroad can damage domestic reputation and goodwill.

Value Risks

Whether the rationale is cost savings or business transformation, an outsourcing project is undertaken to create value for the BPO buyer. With the myriad uncertainties inherent in any complex BPO deal, extracting anticipated value can be a challenge. This risk can be mitigated through several techniques, most of which center on managing the projected outcomes. For example, if the outsourcing deal is expected to save the BPO buyer $1 million in the first year, the PMT should manage to that figure. Adding extra people or hiring consulting firms may be a temptation as project difficulties mount. But this temptation can be resisted if the PMT is committed to hitting the cost-savings targets established for the project.

Another technique for mitigating project value risks is to empower the PMT to constantly seek opportunities to leverage the competencies that develop between the buyer and vendor firms. This tactic, often referred to as *pressing the value model*, will expand the reach of vendor competencies as well as those jointly developed through the BPO relationship. For example, firms that outsource payroll may find that additional advantages can be gained by turning over other back-office functions to the same vendor. When the PMT presses the value model, it seeks to identify other noncore processes that may be suitable for outsourcing under an existing buyer–vendor relationship umbrella.[16] Value risks are inherent in any project as people strive to work together to achieve future organizational states. Working with international vendors presents higher-value risks than does working with domestic vendors in that the extent of potential value is often overstated by the foreign vendor and can take longer than expected to achieve. Mitigation of these risks centers on the effectiveness of SLA negotiation, implementation, and management. Some international vendors have adopted extreme value–risk mitigation tactics to ensure that project deliverables meet expectations. The following case study describes how a lead generation service mitigates this risk.

CASE STUDY

Tele-SalesForce Minimizes Risks through Extensive Quality Control

Tele-SalesForce (TSF) helps U.S. companies outsource their lead generation processes to a call center in Calcutta, India. Chad Burmeister and Tathagata Dasgupta are co-founders of the company, based in Irvine, California. In less than one year of operation, TSF has signed up more than 21 clients. Customers range from major companies such as PeopleSoft and Sun Microsystems to small start-ups.

TSF was launched with the clear goal of providing value in all aspects of a client's lead generation process. The TSF team works with new

---

clients to identify their needs. Following a carefully-designed, step-by-step process, TSF helps clients develop a script for the India-based call-center agents to use when talking to prospects. Prior to actually getting on the phone, each call-center agent assigned to the client role-plays the script and potential prospect responses.

For example, an agent was assigned with acquiring leads from consumer packaged goods (CPG) companies who supply products to Wal-Mart. The agent who was assigned to make those calls did not have any idea what Wal-Mart was, what a CPG company was, or how it works in the United States. Additionally, the agent had no comprehension of how enterprise software application programs could help these companies.

TSF developed a training program for the agent that explained the relationships to the agent in terms of stores and manufacturers that she was familiar with in India. The TSF project manager explained the business relationships and chemistry, what an application can do in the middle of all this, and why she would be calling the decision makers of those companies. This education and the resulting conviction in her voice turned a campaign from getting two leads per *week* into three leads per *day*. This attention to detail helps minimize errors and enhances the chances for a successful call.

In addition to TSF's careful planning to minimize risks, its call-center partner in Calcutta is equally committed to quality performance. A five-year-old company, the India call center used the services of Ernst & Young at its founding to ensure that it installed best practices call-center technologies and procedures. The firm maintains its quality edge by getting regular check ups from E&Y.

Tele-SalesForce is anticipating sales in excess of $1 million for 2005, with growth projected to reach over $7 million by 2008. With the risk-mitigation approach the company is taking to call-center outsourcing, it stands a strong chance of meeting and even exceeding its own growth expectations.

The project management plan can also be an important tool for mitigating value risk because it specifies tasks and responsible parties that can be held accountable on a one-to-one basis. Critical process flows should not be allowed to linger out of compliance for long periods without explanation and plans for remedy. The PMT should have provisions in place for emergency meetings in the event that value goals are not being reached.

Force Majeure Risks

Force majeure risks are the most difficult to quantify and specify. What is the likelihood of a war? A hurricane? An earthquake? No one really knows. Yet these risks can be estimated with some measure of objectivity, and an appropriate mitigation strategy can be developed and enacted.

Planning for Political Unrest

Global geopolitical realities have brought the threat of war to nearly every doorstep. At the same time, reasonable assessments of the probability of war affecting a BPO vendor can be made. Business Monitor International provides extensive coverage of the political, economic, and military risks that exist for countries around the world. Its Web site (*www.businessmonitor.com*) provides a starting place for assessing the war risk associated with the home country of the BPO vendor. Another great source of country-specific information is the U.S. Department of State Web site (*www.state.gov*). It has extensive information for travelers and businesspeople that can help them determine the risks associated with regions worldwide. The PMT can manage its own exposure to liability by utilizing objective information sources in the development of its force majeure risk management plan.

The potential for political unrest exists in many countries that are desirable outlets for outsourcing, such as India and the Philippines. Firms outsourcing to foreign countries should plan for the possibility of war

SARS and the Importance of Planning

The outbreak of severe acute respiratory syndrome (SARS) affected several companies that outsourced functions, especially those based in China. But the effects of SARS were felt in the United States, too.

Companies that had employees working in China when the SARS outbreak occurred had to move those employees back to the United States or have them quarantined. In addition, companies in the United States that received packages from China were concerned about opening them in case the disease could spread.

The SARS outbreak illustrates the importance of planning for unusual and unexpected events. Companies need to understand the flow of their business and how each function or operation could be affected by an unusual event.

and the impact such a conflict would have on their business. Contingency plans should account for a worst-case scenario that would address questions such as:

- What would you do if the country were attacked?
- How would you perform the outsourced functions?
- How would you protect your facility and its contents and your IP?
- Where would you relocate your business?

Planning for Disaster and Recovery

If they have not already, companies that outsource overseas need to develop disaster recovery and business continuity plans. Such plans force organizations to examine possible risks and are crucial if the outsourcing firm wants to purchase insurance to cover property, liability, or business interruption exposures. Also, it is a good idea to have a backup in place in case anything goes wrong with infrastructure, business partners, or distribution channels. In addition to a backup, BPO buyers should consider drawing up a contract with the company responsible for securing the outsourcing. The terms of the contract and the shifting of the risk can be governed by that document. Exhibit 7.3 provides some standard language that can be used to designate vendor responsibilities with respect to disaster recovery planning.

EXHIBIT 7.3

Sample Language for Disaster Recovery

Scope and Definition

The outsourcer shall develop and implement a plan for the prevention and mitigation of business interruptions due to natural and other causes. The outsourcer shall make all reasonable efforts to prevent and recover from such events to ensure the continuity of business operations.

Outsourcer Responsibilities

Make all reasonable efforts to ensure the continuity of operations through implementation of a disaster recovery and business continuity plan. And develop a more detailed and comprehensive plan to ensure business continuity in the event of natural or other events that may cause service, supply chain, delivery, or performance interruptions. The plan must address these activities that are necessary to resume operations at the optimal level at an alternative location within X number of days of a catastrophic event.

Source: "Touch These Bases Before You Sign to Outsource Your IT," *Contractor's Business Management Report* (November 2003): 4–5.

Managing Risks Early

Outsourcing does not mean eliminating business risk; it simply means that some risk is transferred to the BPO vendor. BPO buyers should consider whether they could go back to their old systems if all else failed.[17]

To be effective, an outsourcing deal requires that each partner has considerable benefits to be gained, and that means sharing both risks and rewards. To make that work, the BPO deal must fund the necessary investment and motivate each partner's commitment by aligning goals. Although the financial structure of conventional outsourcing arrangements typically includes bonuses and penalties based on the achievement of minimum service levels by the vendor, the focus of business transformation outsourcing deals is on upside targets. They align incentives around enterprise-level outcomes such as market share and return on equity.[18]

When thinking about using outsourcing, the buyer must also consider the risks it brings to a potential BPO relationship. The BPO provider's readiness to undertake a BPO project is a major determinant of risks to project success. A good starting point to a risk management strategy is for the potential buyer to develop a risk profile of itself. Issues to consider in a risk profile include outsourcing maturity, financial stability, operational capabilities, market goodwill, and access to credit.

Managing risks associated with outsourcing is not unlike managing the risks associated with any other business project. Firms must establish their goals before undertaking the project and then manage to those goals. They must also be aware of the internal and vendor-related HR and change management issues that will arise as a result of launching a BPO project. Each of the various risk factors discussed in this chapter can be managed, but constant attention is required to ensure that problems are addressed before they become unmanageable and that project value is constantly pressed to extract maximal benefit for buyer and vendor alike.

Summary

The risks facing managers and executives in organizations seeking to outsource business processes often go beyond the easily predictable. Defined as those events or conditions that may prevent the BPO organization from achieving its projected benefits, these risks occur in both onshore and offshore environments and can be placed in seven categories: human capital risks, project risks, intellectual property risks, legal risks, vendor organizational risks, value risks, and force majeure risks. It is vital that each of these risks be assessed—at both internal and external levels, as appropriate—and that effective strategies be put in place to anticipate, mitigate, and respond to them as circumstances require. Failure to do so can significantly cripple the potential upside of any BPO initiative.

Endnotes

1. Karl E. Weick and Robert E. Quinn, "Organizational Change and Development," *Annual Review of Psychology* (1999): 361–386.

2. Phillip A. Miscimarra and Kenneth D. Schwartz, "Frozen in Time: The NLRB, Outsourcing, and Management Rights," *Journal of Labor Research* (Fall 1997): 561–580.

3. Roberto Ceniceros, "Moving Operations Overseas Offers Benefits, Challenges," *Business Insurance* (December 22, 2003): 4–5.

4. Lloyd Johnson and Anastasia D. Kelly, "Managing Up, Sideways, and Down," *Corporate Legal Times* (May 2002): 12–13.

5. Mike Bates, "Managing Expectations During ISP Installations," *Law Technology News* (August 2001): 55.

6. Fred Hererra, "Demistifying and Managing Expectations," *Employment Relations Today* (Summer 2003): 21–28.

7. Michael Useem, *Leading Up* (New York: Crown Publishing, 2001).

8. Rick Sturm, "Managing Up: Dealing with an Exec's Technical Shortcomings," *Communications Week* (June 3, 1996): 40.

9. Cade Metz, "Tech Support Coming Home?," *PC Magazine* (February 17, 2004): 20.

10. Lucas Mearian, "Bank Group Offers Guidelines on Outsourcing Security Risks," *Computerworld* (January 26, 2004): 10.

11. Nigel Howard, "Living with the FTC Safeguard Rules: Industry Tips and Experiences," *Investment Lawyer* (September 2003): 1–7.

12. Paul Hurley, "Outsourcing Information Security: Pros Outweigh Cons," *Energy IT* (March/April 2002): 44–47.

13. Robert K. Weiler, "You Can't Outsource Liability for Security," *InformationWeek* (August 26, 2002): 76.

14. Marie Alner, "The Effects of Outsourcing on Information Security," *Information Systems Security* (May/June 2001): 35–43.

15. John Kavanagh, "Split Your Outsourcing Contracts to Guard Against Legal Disputes," *ComputerWeekly* (October 14, 2003): 76.

16. Part of this discussion is derived from the Sourcing Interests Group Research Report.

17. "Touch These Bases Before You Sign to Outsource Your IT," *Contractor's Business Management Report* (November 2003): 4–5.

18. See note 15.

Index